Staying Dry

A Workable
Solution to
the Problem of
Alcohol Abuse

CLAIRE COSTALES

WITH JO BERRY

Regal Books
A Division of GL Publications
Ventura, CA U.S.A.

The foreign language publishing of all Regal books is under the direction of GLINT. GLINT provides financial and technical help for the adaptation, translation, and publishing of books for millions of people worldwide. For information regarding translation contact: GLINT, P.O. Box 6688, Ventura, California 93006.

Formerly published under the title *Alcoholism/The Way Back to Reality*.
Published by Regal Books
A Division of GL Publications
Ventura, California 93006
Printed in U.S.A.

Library of Congress Cataloging in Publication Data
Costales, Claire.
    Staying dry.

    Rev. ed. of: Alcoholism: the way back to reality.
    Includes bibliographical references.
    1. Alcoholics—Rehabilitation.   2. Alcoholism and religion.
I. Berry, Jo.   II. Title.
HB5275.C67   1983   362.2'9386'0926   [B]   83-3417
ISBN 0-8307-0885-5 (pbk.)

For the sake of easier reading, the use of the pronouns, *he, she, him* and *his* in this publication refer for the most part to both male and female in the generic sense.

To my husband Jon, my children Deborah, Dawn and Jon, and to all the alcoholics and their families who allowed me to help them and in doing so helped me to learn and grow and love.

Contents

Acknowledgments

People who are driven by a cause are sometimes hard to cope with—and I'm certainly no exception. GL/Regal Books thought they had been hit by a "white tornado" when I first graced their offices in 1979. I was completely unaware of the impact of my hyper personality until later. But I had a message, and delivering it became the most important thing in the world to me. The people at GL Publications listened. They recognized that there was some potential in Claire Costales, and they patiently began to nurture and disciple me so that I could perform my ministry of warning America about the insidious power of alcohol. I'm sure Regal Books has many authors who are more important, but none have ever felt more special.

I was an unconventional babe in Christ and loved the Lord with all my heart when I finally conquered alcoholism. But, I didn't yet know how to trust God fully in my spiritual growth. What's more, I didn't know where to go to learn about Him. During moments when I had nowhere else to turn I sought help from the people at Regal. By word and example they helped me grow.

Bill Greig, president of GL Publications, and his wife, Doris, taught me acceptance by their living example. For that I love them both. Doris introduced me to the most important help there is—the Holy Bible.

Laurie Leslie is my editor and dear and trusted friend. I love her for her patience and just plain goodness. I can't count how many times she had to tolerate my ignorance and lack of learning. She took time to teach me in quiet, subtle ways and helped me immensely.

Jo Berry, author and Christian teacher, my spiritual

sister, was always available to listen to my personal tor-
ments during withdrawal and to agonize with me
through the first writing of this book.

Then my own family, who had to live with me
through the nightmare years of alcoholism, had to relive
the pain during the writing of *Alcoholism/The Way
Back to Reality,* and this new edition, *Staying Dry.*

At times I have felt abandoned by the Lord, but my
friends assured me that it was I—not the Lord—who
was doing the abandoning. The courage, the strength,
and the growth that took place during the writing of this
book is best described in this beautiful prose by an
unknown author.

One Night I Had A Dream

I dreamed I was walking along the beach with the
Lord, and across the sky flashed scenes from my life.
For each scene I noticed two sets of footprints in the
sand; one belonged to me, the other to the Lord. When
the last scene of my life flashed before us I looked back
at the footprints in the sand. I noticed that many times
along the path of my life, there was only one set of footprints. I also noticed that it happened at the very lowest
and saddest times in my life. I questioned the Lord
about it.

"Lord, you said that once I decided to follow you, you
would walk with me all the way, but I have noticed that
during the most troublesome times in my life, there is
only one set of footprints. I don't understand why in
times when I needed you most, you would leave."

The Lord replied, *"My precious child, I would never
leave you during your times of trial and suffering.
When you see only one set of footprints, it was then
that I carried you."*

Introduction

When I first started working on this book in 1976, I thought I knew a lot about alcoholism. Actually, I knew a lot about the experience of alcoholism, because I had lived through that, but I knew very little about the disease of alcoholism and its residual effects on our lives. As I've continued working in the area of alcohol related problems, I've dissected the problem down to its roots, and what I've discovered about the debilitating impact of alcohol abuse on our society is staggering. There is not one thread of the fabric of this society that isn't frayed by the use of alcohol; the family, the church, educational systems, government, industry, and you, all are affected.

Statistics are usually boring reading, but I urge you to take special note of these which, monumental as they are, underestimate the true picture. The National Institute on Alcoholism and Alcohol Abuse states, "There are at least 100,000 deaths related to alcohol each year."[1] They further verify that at least 26,000 of these mishaps are highway fatalities. This year alone, 875,000 people will be arrested for driving under the influence. I'm told that only .1 of 1 percent of drunk drivers are ever arrested. That puts a possible two and one half million drunk drivers on the road every single day of the year. Experts estimate that in Los Angeles County, at any given moment, one out of ten cars on the road is operated by a drunk driver.

The more I learn the more appalled I am at the enormity of the problem. There is no crevice on this earth that has been sheltered from the effects of alcohol. We cannot stand idly by and do nothing. We must educate ourselves and take positive steps to eradicate the disease. We have to get rid of the negative picture we have of alcoholics so that they can come out of the closet and ask for help and receive treatment. We have to realize that nice mommies and daddies and good sons and daughters, executives and professionals of all kinds, even the clergy, are not exempt from this disease. We have to get the image of the skid row bum out of our heads—only 5 percent of all alcoholics end up on skid row. The rest of them are "respectable citizens," who hide their problem.

I discovered that one major characteristic of alcoholism is secrecy. This comes from the shame you feel at being an alcoholic or having one in your family. Society has cast a black mark against the lowly alcoholic, so most people would rather die than admit they have a problem with drinking. They stay isolated out of fear of reprisal or just out of pure shame.

Consider this: Even if you don't have someone in your family who is addicted to alcohol, every time you leave your home and drive your car you are a potential victim of alcoholism because you are at the mercy of that drunk driver whose car becomes a lethal weapon. Recent statistics show that "alcohol figured in fifty-three percent of California's 5,170 traffic deaths in 1981. The CHP [California Highway Patrol] said in its fourth annual report on traffic accidents that among drivers involved in fatal accidents, ages 21 through 24, almost half had been drinking."[2]

During my early, naive days of recovery I was determined to tackle the whole problem and alter it single-handedly. It didn't seem to me that anybody was working on solving this life-shattering problem. Or, if anyone *was* doing anything it was not having much of an impact. Ignorantly, I felt at the very least I could do a much better job in the area of creating public awareness. Surely, more could be done than was being done at the time. As a Christian I believed I should go to the churches. I thought that all I would have to do would be to call them and offer my services and I would be welcomed with open arms to come and share my message. That was my first mistake! Nine out of ten churches I called politely put me off. Some of them stated that no one in their congregation has "this" problem. That was a big surprise to me. I don't know where they were getting their statistics because my experience and the facts I have collected show otherwise. Christians, including ministers and priests and even nuns—yes, nuns—suffer from alcoholism. Alcohol addiction has no prejudice toward race, creed, color, or position. To believe otherwise is self-destructive.

There are also those who are addicted to tranquilizers or other types of medication who have the same addictive type personality. Only the substance they use is different. Any mind-altering drug is poison to those of us with an addictive nature. Many of us, especially women, go to our doctors with a drug abuse problem and find that the medical profession puts down our complaints and symptoms as female emotionalism. ⌐ome doctors, in fact, compound the problem by prescribing additional tranquilizers or other addictive drugs to "calm" us. Other doctors treat patients while they themselves are under the influence of alcohol.

Time after time I heard from my doctors, "There is nothing wrong with you that a pill won't fix." As I researched this subject from every angle I found that this kind of appeasement attitude is common. We must realize that all drugs are potentially dangerous. And I'm not referring just to women now, I'm talking to each one of you. *Find out about the drug your doctor is prescribing for you!* Ask for manufacturer information about the medication. Don't feel intimidated or that you are disrespectful for asking the doctor what effect, both immediate and long-term, the chemical can have on your body. Ask him questions such as: Will I have to withdraw from the drug? What are its side effects? How long has it been on the market? What is it supposed to do for me? These are some of the most important questions anyone should ask and their answers can save a lot of misery.

If your doctor is critical of your questions or doesn't seem responsive to your problem, find one who is sensitive to the problem. If he treats you like you are stupid when you question him, ask if he personally has ever taken the drug. Chances are he has not. Again, if you have any doubts as to the validity of your treatment, get another opinion. There are doctors out there who do care. They will take time to explain to you about your medication and treatment and won't put you down for asking.

I'm not sure that any mind-altering drugs—such as

tranquilizers, pain pills, sleeping pills and anti-depressants—are safe over a long term. I had numerous doctors assure me that the Valium they were prescribing for me was not addictive. If you have seen the latest information on Valium, you know that it is highly addictive, with extremely dangerous withdrawal symptoms such as convulsions and long-term mental defects.

Again, I say, if you think you are immune to the perils of alcohol and drug abuse because you don't drink or take any medications, please consider the financial burden all of us bear. In 1978 our national public and private expenditures on alcohol related problems was 60 billion dollars, with 20 billion for health care costs alone. According to the National Council on Alcoholism, alcohol abuse and alcoholism drain the economy of an estimated 15 billion dollars annually, with 10 billion dollars for loss of work time in business, industry, civilian professions, government, and the military. Each problem drinker costs his or her company 25 percent of their salary annually.

Consider next the human waste from alcohol use. Brilliant brains, frequently those of teenagers who will shape the future of the world, are being pickled in alcohol. Their brain cells are being destroyed and can never be regenerated. More than 100 million persons in the United States drink alcoholic beverages. Of these, approximately nine million, or one in twelve, develop the disease of alcoholism. Alcoholism is not a crime. It is a disease that can be treated and controlled through education and public awareness. It is to that end that I am writing this book.

Notes
1. *Valley Daily News,* September 10, 1982, Sect. 1, p. 4.
2. Ibid.

one
A Career in Alcoholism

Booze has always plagued mankind. Down through the ages there have always been people who could not or would not resist the fruit of the vine—who chose to pursue the career of alcoholism.

I am fully aware that alcoholism is a disease but, based on my own experience, I know it is also a chosen life's work. The alcoholic chooses drinking for his profession. He may not say, "I am going to be a drinker," the way someone would say, "I want to be a doctor," or "I'm going to be a secretary." But at some point in time he decides that this is what he wants to be. Then, like anyone who has decided what career he will pursue, he directs all of his energy toward achieving and reaching that goal.

His choice of this particular career is influenced by

many factors: the type of person he is; concepts he is exposed to; seeing drinking presented as a different, pleasant, challenging career opportunity.

The media bombard us with the idea that drinking is fun. Ever watch the barroom scenes in a beer advertisement on television? Everyone is friendly. The men are "macho" and the women are appealing.

We are also brainwashed into believing that beautiful people drink. Take a minute to examine closely the liquor ads in magazines. The women are strikingly pretty, the men handsome. They are dressed in expensive, fashionable clothes and the background is a romantic setting. They look happy, content and in perfect control of the situation. This kind of advertising encourages people to drink, especially people with the disease of alcoholism.

The Career Begins Early

The predominant element in choosing a career is parental opinion and family tradition. People tend to act out what is modeled for them. If a child lives in a home where drinking is an incorporated part of his existence, statistics prove he will probably drink.

Children cannot discern what is right or wrong, good or bad, unless they are told and taught. When a child sees one or both parents drinking, socializing over booze, offering liquor to guests, spending money on it, he will assume, because his mother and father are doing these things, that alcohol is good and it is all right to drink.

At the same time, he is taught that liquor is not good for children so he anticipates that great moment when he takes a step into adulthood and imbibes for the first time. If he starts when he is too young, his parents may chew him out or punish him, but ultimately he knows they can't say too much because they drink themselves. It is just a matter of time until he too drinks regularly and often.

That's why I picked alcoholism for my career. I made up my mind when I was quite young that I was going to be a drinker. Oh, it wasn't a conscious, tangible decision but rather an internal commitment and a secret desire to use booze.

When I was growing up I developed a positive attitude toward drinking because of the way it was presented to me in my home. I saw it as something worth pursuing. We are Irish and there was always a bountiful supply of good Irish whiskey on hand for every occasion.

My family drank to celebrate. I have warm memories of the people I love drinking, laughing, sharing, being happy and singing together around the piano. When business was transacted, the deal was inevitably sealed with a toast. Hospitality included offering our guests a drink.

When someone died, my family drank at the wake to help them get through the ordeal. I remember enjoying the drink of whiskey and lemon I was given when I was sick. On another occasion I remember a whiskey soaked piece of cotton being laid on my sore tooth to relieve the pain. My mother was as kind and good a person as you would ever want to meet, and this alcohol was administered out of love and affection. She never drank alcohol as a beverage but only used it for medicinal purposes; in doing so, she innocently put her seal of approval on booze. I was taught by example that booze helps everything—that it is the best cure-all around; a panacea for whatever ails you.

Pursuing the Career: The First Drink
As a child I had many opportunities to taste liquor

and beer because it was used frequently in my home. I had five brothers and they all drank. Much of the time they were mellow and sometimes melancholy, but at other times they were aggressive, even violent, with one another. You would think that a child who was reared in this kind of environment would never drink when she grew up. Let me tell you the other side of that logic. I remember my brothers being so much fun when they had had a few drinks in them. They would always give me money and attention. The affection I craved from those heroes of mine was in my eyes a benefit of the booze. Liquor helped me get what I wanted. So when I left home at the age of seventeen I left behind all negative memories and feelings and retained only the pleasant ones.

Drinking represented excitement and sophistication to me, a truly "grown-up" experience. The media bombards us with the concept, *Make Your Life Better with Booze.* They show us positive, beautiful people who look successful and happy and are enjoying life to the fullest. I assumed that really neat people drank. Everything I associated with being socially acceptable included having booze. So, that association, along with the frequent "tastes" I had as a child, helped me to look forward to my first drink with great anticipation. It was like a reward or prize to me. There were a whole lot of emotional strings attached to that first full drink.

I'm sure now that subconsciously I viewed drinking as a free ride into adulthood without having to live through the painful day-to-day process of growing up. I thought that the minute I got that drink into me, I would appear sophisticated and grown-up to everybody. That's exactly how I pictured myself. Little did I know that the rest of the world saw me as a little girl who was making a fool of herself by drinking too much. Not cool. Not positive. But I never looked for or listened to anyone's opinion. I was certain I knew what I was doing.

The Alcoholic Personality

I know now that I chose alcoholism for my career because of the kind of person I am. Just as a teacher has a built-in desire to impart knowledge and a doctor has a compulsion to heal, I had a predisposition for alcohol. As I've talked with medical experts and interviewed alcoholics I've discovered that problem drinkers possess a distinctive combination of personality traits and, quite possibly, an inherited tendency toward the disease. We have what I would call an "alcoholic personality."

What unmanageable combination of characteristics make up this alcoholic personality?

The first characteristic is *anxiety, being constantly tense and fearful for no reason.* In my own life, the liquor dissolved that ever-present, unreasonable knot of fear that made its home in the pit of my stomach. I was so accustomed to being anxious and uptight that the glow I got gave me a false courage and a pseudo self-confidence I had never experienced before. I thought I had found the key to heaven!

Next, there is *dissatisfaction*—malaise; being generally unhappy and discontent. This kind of person is never quite satisfied with who he is or his station in life, but he is unable to pinpoint any specific reason for his uneasiness.

Because a person with this type of personality is dissatisfied, he is also *retaliatory*—defensive, quick-tempered and vengeful. He lashes out with no provocation and fights back, even when retreating would be the easiest and best course of action. Eventually, he retaliates by drinking.

Another characteristic is *frustration*. Numerous

alcoholics I have talked with claim they were hyperactive children. Usually people outgrow this condition, but in someone who has an alcoholic personality, this agitation intensifies with age.

As an adult the problem drinker is unsettled, constantly spinning his wheels but getting nowhere fast. He is seldom, if ever, tranquil but since he cannot release his frustrations by doing the things children do, such as hitting, kicking, name-calling or screaming, he chooses the socially acceptable way to calm his nerves. He drinks.

The alcoholic personality is also *emotionally detached.* Although he isn't necessarily what you would call a "loner," he is remote. He chooses not to reveal himself and is uninvolved in the everyday affairs of others. He is not uncaring but is a solitary soul who separates himself from the concerns and criticisms of others by building a wall of detachment. As a result, he cannot contribute in meaningful ways to interpersonal relationships.

Because he isolates himself emotionally, he neither listens nor responds to advice. It isn't that he doesn't care; he simply is not tuned in. His aloofness costs him the approval he so desperately needs because, in spite of his I-don't-give-a-damn attitude, he inordinately wants to please and be loved and accepted. Then when he is rejected, he drinks to soothe the hurt.

A final personality trait of the career alcoholic is *dishonesty.* He is deceitful and lies both to himself and others. Many times he feels forced to, to cover his drinking. He also fantasizes and manipulates to get what he wants.

Psychologists claim that we all fantasize. Most people's illusions are harmless daydreams but an alcoholic substitutes bizarre mental imaginings for reality, creating a world of his own; a sort of psychic limbo where he invents his version of truth and responds to it as he chooses.

The alcoholic needs the stimulation of alcohol to help him live in his created fantasies so that he doesn't have to look at life truthfully and realistically. When working with alcoholics, the first step is to penetrate that fantasy, giving them a taste of reality.

A person with this kind of personality is a master manipulator. Everett L. Shostrom, author of *Man the Manipulator,* defines a manipulator as "a person who exploits, uses and/or controls himself and others as things in certain self-defeating ways."[1] He observes that, "Above all, a manipulator wants no one, not even loved ones, to learn his deeper feelings."[2]

Why is it necessary for an alcoholic to engage in this form of manipulation and dishonesty? There are basically three reasons.

First, he manipulates to control his circumstances and other people so that they will say and do certain things that will bring about the reaction he wants. Then he can use their behavior as an excuse for his drinking. *An alcoholic will use anyone and do anything to get a drink.* If he has to cheat, lie, steal or mistreat someone in order to get his supply and structure his face-saving excuses, then he will. But he has discovered that instead of overtly doing these things, it is more expedient and comfortable for him if he does them underhandedly.

Second, he manipulates to hide his feelings. He does not want anyone to know what makes him tick, because if they did then he would be vulnerable to them and he could not use them. He isolates himself emotionally so no one has an opportunity to see him as he is; therefore they respond to what he appears to be.

Finally, he manipulates to justify his drinking, to create a viable, visible reason for his overindulgence. He contrives situations that prevent people from approaching him in positive, constructive ways, then drinks to drown his invented hurts.

To an alcoholic, lying isn't morally wrong, it is merely personally comfortable and expedient. Eventually, the drinker is trapped in the ultimate lie: He says, "I am not an alcoholic," then keeps on drinking to prove he can handle liquor.

New information has recently been documented by medical researchers proving that there are two kinds of alcoholism which I will call type A and type B. Type A is related to the genetic predisposition to the disease such as I have. Type B results from the misuse or abuse of drugs or alcohol.

When you suppress emotional discomfort artificially with booze, because it's easier to live in oblivion than face reality, pretty soon you may forget why you started using the drug in the first place. Then what becomes important is staying oblivious. The original problem becomes secondary, if it is present at all.

Let me give you a typical example of a type B alcoholic. An elderly, retired gentleman I know had an illustrious career, was well-known in his profession, was an outstanding Christian and community leader, and never imbibed in more than an intermittent glass of wine at an occasional business dinner. He never drank in front of his wife or children. He was what I would call a "solid citizen."

Two years ago this nice gentleman, whom I'll call Peter, encountered a traumatic situation. His wife was diagnosed as having terminal cancer. She suffered terribly for one year before her death. It has been a little over a year since she died and presently Peter is a full-fledged alcoholic. This sensible man under normal circumstances would never have been attracted to or gotten hooked on alcohol. But under this tremendous stress he started using booze as a tranquilizer to temporarily soothe his grief. He had none of the personality traits of an alcoholic to start with but, after only one year of use, ended up possessing all of the characteristics of someone who was born with those traits.

The Environment Factor

Will everyone who possesses this combination of attributes become an alcoholic? No one can say absolutely, but the odds strongly indicate that they will. Certainly environment plays a part in the development of the alcoholic personality and can act as either a deterrent or a contributing factor.

In my case, my environment fostered such a personality. I was always a worrier but no one showed me how to conquer my fears. From childhood I was retaliatory and a habitual liar; but either no one noticed or they didn't take the time to correct me. I was a nervous, hyperactive child with an overabundance of energy; unsettled and belligerent.

Being the last of ten children, I had a "caboose" complex. Badly as I wanted to be a part of the mainstream of things, I was positionally—and soon became emotionally—detached. I just got lost in the crowd. My brothers and sisters thought I was spoiled because I got away with a lot. But the reason I did was because no one really noticed what I did. I was ignored and felt neglected.

Perhaps if this composite of traits had been recognized as a destructive element when I was young, the pattern could have been broken. As with any disease, early detection increases the chances for a cure.

If I had learned *before* I started drinking how to cope with stress and fear, how to channel my energy, how to

be honest and open rather than deceitful and manipulative, I probably would not have become an alcoholic. If
only one link in the chain of my alcoholic personality
had been severed, if I had been taught the importance of
separating fact from fantasy, and if booze hadn't been
presented to me as acceptable, helpful and glamorous,
chances are I would not have chosen a career in alcoholism.

If the characteristics discussed in this chapter are
descriptive of you or someone you know, child or adult,
he or she is a potential alcoholic who needs help in overcoming these personality traits. A vital element in both
the prevention and recovery from this disease is recog-
nizing these symptoms early enough to avoid addiction
to any substance.

Just a few weeks ago my husband, Jon, and I were
watching one of the exhibition, pre-season football
games on television. I became extremely uncomfort-
able. I realized I was tense because I was being bom-
barded by beer ads. When the sponsors were not cutting
away to convince us it was "time to relax," they were
informing us if we said, "Bud," we'd said it all. We
counted twenty-one specific promotions to use booze in
the time it took to play the game. There was not so
much as one reference to the prevention of alcoholism.

If you compare the amount of prevention coverage
to the number of beer ads, you will have a sad awakening. The amount of money spent on making those ads
can never be matched by the present, feeble attempts at
promoting prevention. I am glad to say that the NIAAA
(National Institute on Alcoholism and Alcoholic Abuse)
has recently put together a fabulous ad in affiliation with
one of the most important public relations firms in the
country. It is geared toward the drunk driver and shows a
young man and woman sitting on the beach. She is talk-

ing about the aspirations of her life. "I want to go to Venice. I want to write a novel," she confides. The message is that she loses those dreams, as well as her life, to a drunk driver.

There was as much money and effort poured into that ad as in any about a drinking product. I am convinced this kind of advertising can be done if the public demands it. If ads for prevention of alcoholism could be given equal time in the media, their presentation could have a tremendous effect. They would help balance the false input the public receives from liquor manufacturers. I feel sure it would alter the statistics.

I have no delusions about getting alcohol banned in our society, but since we are always going to be dealing with this problem, I suggest we educate ourselves about it. Unless we do, this epidemic could literally destroy the very fibers of our society. This very day ten million Americans are known to have the disease of alcoholism. I think that warrants our attention. Also, every alcoholic affects, and sometimes destroys, the lives of at least three other human beings—wives, husbands, children, parents, innocent victims—which brings the number of Americans who presently are suffering in some way from the effects of alcoholism to forty million. What on earth will it take to force us to make a realistic appraisal of the wreckage and desolation left in the path of alcoholism?

We are becoming so desensitized to the problems that exist in our world that words don't have much impact. We are tuned out to the pain of others. I am as guilty as anyone. I was reminded of this while watching the Jerry Lewis muscular dystrophy telethon this past Labor Day. The television set had been on for quite a while and I wasn't actually watching the program. I was taking care of some of the paperwork for my foundation, but every now and then someone would catch my attention. Each time he or she was asking for money. I remember getting very irritated. I caught myself mumbling aloud, "I have enough trouble trying to handle my own financial obligations." I wasn't concerned with the kid who had died since last year's telethon because a cure hadn't been found. I didn't care that the dedicated people in that organization had done terrific work and that their cause truly deserved my dollar. Instead, I was angry with them for making me feel guilty! Can you believe that?

In much the same way, we are indifferent to the problem of alcoholism in our society. We would rather pretend it didn't exist; then we wouldn't have to do anything about it. I have seen teenagers wearing T-shirts advertising beer or whiskey. I have seen little children and infants wearing Coors hats or shorts. This year our local alcohol advisory board sent me a copy of an ad for a new candy. It is a miniature replica of a Budweiser can. The candy is called "older but wiser." That is a disgrace. It encourages our youth to view beer as something tasty and a fun thing to do. It glorifies drinking.

Environment can be changed. Personalities can be altered or remolded. If potential or stricken victims are identified and treated it is possible to divert them from a career in alcoholism.

Notes
1. Everett L. Shostrom, *Man the Manipulator* (New York: Bantam Books, 1968), p. xii.
2. Ibid., p. 5.

two
The "If Only" Excuses

The two men obviously were skid row bums. You could tell they had gotten dressed up for the television interview. Their clothes were unkempt and mismatched but clean. Both looked about sixty. I was shocked when one said he was forty-two and the other forty-four.

In the course of the conversation, one of them revealed that he was a college graduate with an advanced degree in electronics. Surprised, the host of the show asked him why he had ended up on skid row. His reply? "Well, *if only* I hadn't lost my job in the early sixties and my wife hadn't left me, I wouldn't be here now."

If only. Most people, at some time in their lives, rationalize; we all indulge in the "I did it because" routine. We feel it is necessary at times to explain to ourselves, to justify what we do and explain why we do it. We want to be validated and understood. Frequently, for our own peace of mind and to salve our consciences, we need to establish what we think are acceptable reasons for behaving as we do.

In the alcoholic this process is pronounced. All drinkers rationalize. They invent what I call *if-only* excuses that supply them with what they believe are legitimate reasons for drinking.

Let me illustrate how an *if only* works. Let's say my husband calls and says he has been detained at a business meeting and will be an hour late getting home. This throws me completely because I cannot cope with the change in routine, so I take a few drinks. I rationalize, "*If only* Jon would have come home on time I wouldn't have taken those drinks." In actuality, what I did was use the fact that my husband was coming home late as an excuse for drinking.

Yes, we alcoholics need our *if onlys.* They are a manipulative device we use to force reactions from others so we can create drinking situations. *If onlys* are a clever ploy drinkers subconsciously use to victimize others and relieve their own responsibility. Quite simply, we set ourselves up as punching bags, dare others to hit us, and when they do we drink because we've been struck.

Based on my experience, I have identified five *if onlys* that alcoholics use to perpetuate their behavior.

If Only Things Were Different
(escape from reality)

I used to think that if everything and everyone around me would change, if the world and the people in it would improve or do what I thought they should, then I wouldn't drink. I was evading reality. "If only things were different" is an escape mechanism for an alcoholic. He uses it because he needs a scapegoat, someone or something to blame; so he lays the responsibility for his problems at the feet of people or situations over which he seemingly has no control.

Many times I kidded myself by blaming other people for what I was doing to myself. My drinking problem was *their* fault. *If only* "they" would change, then I could quit drinking. I remember I deluded myself into believing that my husband's attitude toward me made me drink, when actually his attitude was a reaction to my drinking. And I was convinced that the pressure of raising three little kids was also a cause. I decided my children were harder to handle than other women's were. So I said, "*If only* my children were calm, well-behaved, and soft-spoken, then I wouldn't drink." I desperately needed a reason. I was willing to blame my own son and daughters for my inadequacies. I had to have my *if only* or face the insanity of alcohol.

"If only things were different" is a lie in two ways. First, an alcoholic would not stop drinking if things were different. Circumstances change constantly yet he still drinks. When he is happy he drinks because he feels good. When his mood changes he drinks because he's sad or depressed. If he gets a raise or a promotion he celebrates by getting drunk. And he gets drunk if he is demoted or gets fired. He drinks regardless of how things are.

Second, this excuse is dishonest because it is a way of evading reality. The alcoholic will not accept life as it is. He avoids basic truths such as the fact that life is hard, is not fair, that there are people who will reject or dislike him, and that he will always have problems. They are part of the human condition.

Dr. Manuel J. Smith, in his book *When I Say No I Feel Guilty,* puts it this way: "No matter what you or I do, other people can cause problem after problem. Many of us have the unrealistic belief that having to live with problems day after day is an unhealthy or unnatural life-style. Not so! It is entirely natural."[1]

My personal way of eliminating this *if only* was to step back into reality. I did that by writing down the things that hurt me, by recording on paper the feelings and frustrations I was experiencing. I must admit I used some pretty strong language and penned some harsh facts, but it worked.

For example, if I was angry at my husband, if I started thinking, *"If only* Jon was different," I would sit down and write pages and pages, exploding on paper, telling him how I felt, what a rotten guy he was and what my struggles were. I'd lay it all out, every nasty detail, then I would read it aloud. To me, that was the same as saying it to him face to face. Finally, I would set fire to the paper and watch my hurts, anger, bitterness, and frustrations evaporate into smoke. I substituted honest communication, listing the way things actually were, for a drink.

For me, writing acted as a catharsis. It helped me put things into perspective, decide what I needed to verbalize and what I needed to keep to myself. It also helped me discern which of my thoughts were irrational and inappropriate.

Every alcoholic must realize that: (1) *if only* things were different their circumstances might be worse instead of better; (2) external changes will not stop him from drinking; (3) problems are a part of life that cannot be drowned in alcohol. Ultimately, the one sure way any alcoholic can make things different is by not drinking.

If Only This Hadn't Happened
(self-pity)
I think I said this second *if only* more than anyone

else in the world. I was literally drowning in self-pity. I would moan, "Why me? Why should I get all the bad breaks?" I was so busy feeling sorry for myself— because I was the last child born into the family, because I had been rejected by a friend, because I was bored, because, because, because—that I didn't have enough energy left to do anything constructive, such as respond to those who loved me or to help myself.

"If only this hadn't happened to me" is related to the inconsequential, everyday happenings in life. The alcoholic cannot emotionally handle even minor upsets. It's not like someone died or there has been a great tragedy; he caves in if someone snaps at him, if a department store clerk doesn't respond to him immediately, if his wife fixes chicken instead of steak, if one of the children walks in front of the TV set when he's watching a program, if he has a flat tire.

He blows out of proportion everything that happens so that he can use it as a cause for self-pity. *If only* he wasn't married to Sally, or if he had gotten there sooner, or later, or not at all. *If only* life hadn't happened to him, then he wouldn't be an alcoholic.

I used to bemoan the fact that I was the tenth child, so I dwelt on *if only* I'd been the first, or third, or even fifth. I know a young lady who is adopted and her cop-out is, "*If only* my natural parents had wanted me. *If only* I belonged." The truth is, her adoptive parents deeply loved and wanted her; but that is irrelevant to her because she needs "*if only* I weren't adopted" as an excuse for drinking.

Part of my recovery process was learning to look at what I was doing to myself that was causing my misery instead of looking at what others were doing to me or what was happening to me. When I started facing reality I realized that I was causing most of my problems and that the ones I didn't cause were magnified by my drinking. I asked God to help me see life from His perspective. Things look much better when you are looking down from heaven rather than up from the pit of hell. I asked the Lord to make me aware of positive things that were taking place.

I talked to myself, I told myself, out loud, how good certain things were, how pleasant and productive life could be. Now, I look for positives rather than negatives, I see good even in the bad. I have a new, exciting appreciation for people.

Before, when I was moaning, "If only this hadn't happened to me," I was suffering under the burden of motherhood. Now, I am awestruck at the wonder and love of my children. They have every reason to hate me, but they don't. They have found me passed out on the couch when they arrived home from school. They have seen me make a fool of myself many times while I was drinking. They witnessed not one but three suicide attempts. They had to bury their little heads under their pillows to avoid hearing the screaming fights Jon and I had about my drinking. They were disrupted out of a sound sleep more nights than I care to remember when, in my drunken stupor, I dragged them from their beds, wanting to take them and leave.

The children never said a bad word about me. All they knew was that I was their mother and they loved me. You can imagine that if they loved me when I was in that condition, now they are faithful, loving children beyond my wildest dreams. As we have talked at length about my problem, I've learned they understood it even before I did. Gratitude and optimism have replaced my debilitating self-pity.

If Only I Could Control What Is Happening
(self-delusion)

The third *if only* is an insidious cancer in the soul. The alcoholic believes that if he can control his circumstances and people's reactions to him, his drinking problem will vanish. He thinks that *if only* everybody liked him, treated him fairly, accepted him as he is, and never criticized him or made demands on him *then* he would not have reason to drink.

So, in order to control others—to make them like him, treat him fairly and accept him—he tries to be all things to all people. He becomes a people pleaser.

I would let people use and abuse me in hopes that they would be nice to me if I pleased them. I thought if I did what they wanted, they would, in return, do what I wanted; I could control what happened if I did what everyone required of me. It didn't work! I was deluding myself. I tried to be all things to all people and became a first-class hypocrite instead.

I could never figure out why people didn't do what I wanted when I was willing to compromise myself to get a favorable response. The harder I tried, the more frustrated I became, the more I drank and the less control I had over what was happening. I know now I was afraid of managing my own life and of accepting responsibility for my mistakes, so I unknowingly submitted myself to the influence and whims of others. Consequently, I was discontented because I was utterly at their mercy.

Dr. Wayne Dyer suggests that "learning to take total charge of yourself will involve a whole new thinking process ... [because] you've probably grown up believing that you can't control your own emotions ... [but] feelings are reactions you choose to have. If you are in charge of your own emotions you don't have to choose self-defeating reactions."[2]

Families of alcoholics frequently suffer from this *if only,* too. They desperately want to control what is happening: to make the drinker stop drinking, to speak the magic word or perform the miraculous deed that will make him give up the bottle. So they plead, beg, cajole, nag, and condemn, which makes him drink more. What they and the alcoholic need to accept is that they can control what is happening only if they control themselves. Self-control is as far as the scope of anyone's influence goes.

I cannot control another human being nor can he control me *unless consent is given.* When I realized this amazing truth and took charge of my own life, my frustrations and anxieties started disappearing. But I still have a struggle with this. Sometimes I am afraid to tell someone no when I don't want to do something for fear he or she will get angry or not like me. Or, I will too readily accept unfair, unwarranted criticism about myself rather than stand up for myself when I am right. But I am improving.

I am in remission and know I can stay there forever because I am in charge of myself and accept responsibility for what I do and say: *I am responsible for myself and no longer will let others rule me.* I may not be able to control my circumstances but I can control my responses to them, and in that way I control what is happening.

If Only Everyone Would Leave Me Alone (self-destruction)

Alcoholism is a form of suicide. Not only is it physically destructive but the emotions are negatively affected. The drinker is sensitive only to his own addiction, never to the needs of others. He doesn't care whom he hurts, including himself, because he is consumed by his selfish desire to drink.

Alcoholism is socially destructive. Interpersonal relationships are altered and sometimes terminated. The alcoholic's ability and drive to perform are hindered, and eventually stifled altogether. He can neither be a friend nor have any because friends infringe on his "right" to drink. Usually, if an alcoholic is married, the union ends in divorce unless the family gets help in some kind of intervention program or the alcoholic finally realizes that if he doesn't stop he will lose his family. As I said before, the pressure of something stronger than the pressure to drink may bring the alcoholic around. If the family chooses to go for help, what usually happens is they learn how to break the cycle of behavior in the relationship and the alcoholic is left without his excuses. This is when the making or breaking of the relationship occurs.

Alcohol also kills the soul. It is spiritually debilitating. The alcoholic worships and stands in awe of only one thing—booze; and what happens to him when he partakes is not uplifting or edifying but downgrading and humiliating. That is why no alcoholic can recover without turning to God as his Saviour. His idol, liquor, has to be replaced with a God who is alive and who has the power to help him overcome his addiction.

The alcoholic represses the fact that he is killing himself; but those around him, the caring people—especially family and friends—realize what is happening. They understand that he is killing himself by degrees. Being reasonably normal and compassionate, they do not want him to take his life so they try to do what they can to stop him.

If you saw someone with a gun pointed at his temple,

chances are you would try to keep him from pulling the trigger. Those who try to help the alcoholic grab at his bottle, trying to pry it from him so he won't kill himself; but he won't let go.

Suicide is an extremely selfish act. When a person takes his own life he is punishing his family, friends, associates and society in general for failing him, misunderstanding him and neglecting him. He doesn't care whom he hurts or what will be the ramifications of his death after he is gone. Taking his life is his way of getting back at everyone and at the same time escaping reality.

The alcoholic chooses liquor as his death weapon and he does not want anyone to tell him not to drink or to point out what he is doing to himself. He is completely self-centered. He does not care how much anyone suffers as long as he can have his booze. That is the insanity of this kind of self-destruction: *The drink is more important than life.*

I was once convinced that anyone who made remarks about my drinking like, "Come on now, Claire, don't you think you've had enough?" was rude and inconsiderate. That person became my arch enemy. I thanked the person, with a totally defensive response, raging at him in anger. I interpreted his concern as interference. He had no right. It was my business if I wanted to get drunk. To hell with who might get hurt.

The basic reason a drunk wants to be left to his own devices is because, in his sober moments, he feels guilty for what he has done and for hurting those who care about him. Since he does not want to cope with guilt during his lucid moments, he tries to compensate by doing penance to the people he has embarrassed and hurt.

After I'd been on a binge or had been drunk, I would

wake up with a hangover words cannot describe, but the physical discomfort was a minor aspect. The "morning after" was one big, ugly self-hate trip. The first thing that struck me was fear, because I couldn't remember what I'd done the night before. Then I was overcome with guilt. I was a trashy tramp, a selfish slob who did horrible, thoughtless things to the people she loved. I loathed myself.

To "make it up" to my husband and children, I would get up, disguise the physical dissipation with make-up and fix breakfast, nearly killing myself trying to please everybody. How many mothers let every child in the family eat something different for the morning meal? I did. I'd make pancakes for one, hot cereal for another, orange juice for Debbie, chocolate milk for Dawn. All of this while I was barely able to stand the odor or sight of the food.

Of course, Jon was mad that I had stayed out late or came home plastered, but he was wooed by my obvious efforts to please him; so he avoided mentioning what had happened and went off to work with that unspoken barrier between us. Then I'd worry all day about what was going to happen when he came home that night. I knew he would insist on questioning me.

If only he would leave me alone! But I knew he wouldn't so I resorted to a surefire cure for my nerves: I would take a drink because I did not want to think about what I'd done or face the unpleasantness I knew was coming. But we never got around to talking about the night before because by the time Jon got home I was already repeating the pattern: I was drunk.

Many suicide attempts are cries for help. The victim actually does not want to end his life. Experts tell us that when someone truly intends to kill himself he will accomplish the act. Some alcoholics will never stop drinking. Others, like myself, are only *attempting* suicide. When we say, "If only they would leave me alone," we don't mean it. We are crying for help.

Although no one can make an alcoholic stop drinking, a friend or relative can certainly contribute to his recovery just by being there, even when the drinker rejects him. Stubborn, persistent love may help him take that big, important step toward sobriety, when he says, "I need you too," instead of "Leave me alone." That is what saved me: a loving God who pulled me to His heart and a family who refused to give up on me even when I had given up on myself.

If Only I Weren't This Way
(self-degradation)

Generalizations are dangerous because they are absolute and leave no room for exceptions, but I am going to make one: *every alcoholic has a bad self-image,* so bad that he exposes himself in the worst possible light most of the time and consistently puts his worst foot forward. For the alcoholic, drinking is a way of camouflaging the person he is, whom he doesn't like, and either can't or doesn't know how to change.

The alcoholic dislikes himself so intensely that he drinks, makes a fool of himself and sloshes through life in a vat of booze to punish himself. He keeps thinking, *"If only* I weren't this way. *If only* I weren't me." And because he is who he is, he drinks. He would rather die than live with himself the way he is.

The way an alcoholic degrades himself or herself is a highly personal thing. I looked at myself and thought, *I am inadequate. I am a failure. Why can't I be like Susan or Betty?* I wondered, *What's wrong with me? Other women are happy and they are in the same situation I am; young mothers with a house to care for, a husband to satisfy, and a family to raise.* And, because I couldn't live up to the image of what I thought I should be, I drank.

I was convinced that I was an unfit mother and a terrible wife, so that's what I became. I doused myself in liquor to keep from facing who and what I was; but the drug did not make the pain go away. The more I drank, the more I hated myself, the faster my disease progressed, the more turmoil and trauma I experienced. I loathed what I had become.

I decided I was a nothing so I turned into a nothing. But because I wanted to be valued, accepted and loved, I spent years trying to please everybody with whom I came in contact. When I failed (nobody can please everybody all of the time) I drank because I felt sorry for myself and for the people I had let down.

In her book *Can You Love Yourself?* Jo Berry observes, "You're going to love others in the same way you love yourself. You'll treat them in the way you treat yourself. If you don't love yourself you can't love anyone else."[3] The dilemma the alcoholic faces is that, although he desperately wants to love himself, by the time he's a plain old drunk there's not much left to love.

He is externally as well as internally repulsive to himself and probably to others. Contrary to the popular notion, all the world does not love a drunk. They are not funny or cute or the life of the party. They are stinky, rude, and pushy; intrusions into the comfortable flow of life.

I found that the first thing I had to do was to *deprogram all the wrong ideas I had about myself.* I actually asked some friends to write down some things they liked about me. I clung to those lists. They were a life preserver in a stormy sea. I was surprised to find that many of their opinions were totally different from ones I had of myself. I'll never forget how great I felt when one woman (whom I had imposed upon and caused all kinds of embarrassment) said I was good company and a stimulating conversationalist (when I was sober).

Dr. Wayne Dyer calls these self-labels "I'ms." He says the self-defeating ones are the result of the use of four neurotic sentences: "(1) That's me. (2) I've always been that way. (3) I can't help it. (4) That's my nature."[4] And he gives many examples of what happens when people act out these self-labels. My *"if only* I weren't this way" started to disintegrate when I stopped labelling myself a drunk and started calling myself a sober lady.

Oh, there'd be times when I'd slip or be depressed and start thinking of myself as a weak-willed drunk, but I refused to cling to those ideas. H. Norman Wright notes, "We may not always be able to prevent the wrong pictures from flashing on the screen but we don't need to indulge ourselves in the images."[5] So I didn't. I stopped looking at what I was and focused on what I could be.

When I stopped drinking, other people started feeling comfortable around me, enjoying my company and responding to me in positive ways. Now I have actually learned to love myself.

Simply stated, *if onlys* are a facade alcoholics use to keep from facing the fact of their drinking. The only way to eliminate if onlys is by admitting the truth.

The alcoholic must *replace "if only" fantasy phrases with fact.* "This is the way it is," or "I am this kind of person." Family and friends can be of help if they will state factual truths to the problem drinker, keeping reality alive to him. When he is retreating from reality by saying, *"If only* things were different," tell him this is the way things are. He has to learn to verbalize his feelings and he needs a good listener when he does; not a judge but a compassionate mentor.

Rather than drowning in the self-pity of *"If only* this hadn't happened to me," he needs to have someone tell him exactly what is happening in an objective, unemotional manner.

The self-delusion of *"If only* I could control what is happening," should be countered with the truth of, "You are responsible for what you say, do and cause to happen." The alcoholic must surrender his self-destructive weapon, liquor, and realize that everyone would stop harassing him about his drinking if he would quit boozing.

Finally the alcoholic has to *stop degrading himself.* He must quit moaning, *"If only* I weren't this way." He must honestly, openly admit that he is a drunk then acknowledge that, with God's help, he can change that along with all the other things he dislikes about himslf. He must also learn to appreciate the good things about himself. And there *are* many good things about each one of us. All we need to do is look for them.

Loved ones who want to help can do more by programming realistic ideas into the alcoholic's appraisal of himself than they can by nagging him about drinking. For instance, he needs to hear positive truths about himself, such as: You are kind. You have a good sense of humor. You are generous. Or, as in my case, You are a good conversationalist.

He also needs to hear: You are hurting yourself and others. You are too drunk to listen to what I am saying. You are feeling sorry for yourself. Or, you are wasting your potential.

Insanity must be countered with sanity, and destruction with edification. Until the alcoholic can do this for himself, it is up to those around him to do it for him. With persistence, the *if onlys* can be replaced with truth and recovery can begin.

Notes

1. Manuel J. Smith, *When I Say No I Feel Guilty* (New York: The Dial Press, 1975), p. 3.
2. Wayne W. Dyer, *Your Erroneous Zones* (New York: Funk and Wagnalls Co., 1976), p. 9.
3. Jo Berry, *Can You Love Yourself?* (Ventura, CA: Regal Books, 1978), p. 75.
4. Dyer, *Erroneous Zones,* p. 65.
5. H. Norman Wright *The Christian Use of Emotional Power* (Old Tappan, NJ: Fleming H. Revell Co., 1974), p. 32.

three
Staying Dry: The First Steps

When Jo and I started working on this book she asked me what finally made me decide to stop drinking. I told her it depended on which time she meant. The first time it was the fact that I wanted to show everyone that I could quit anytime I wanted. The second time, I wanted to please my husband. Then, it was because of money. This last time I quit out of self-disgust. I had stooped so low and was so sick of myself I couldn't stand being the way I was.

Regardless of the surface motivations, the real reason I swore off the bottle was because some factor became greater than the compulsion to drink. The primary reason any alcoholic quits drinking is because *he seeks to relieve the pressure of alcohol only when another pressure becomes greater and more urgent to his survival.*

It is a common misconception that at some point in time an alcoholic will realize he needs help and that he will then want to stop drinking. That is not true. No alcoholic ever wants to quit nor does he think he has to. He thinks he is the only drunk in the world who can handle his booze. The only reason any alcoholic stops is *because some other factor in his life becomes more demanding than his need to drink.* And if he does quit, in his mind he is doing so only temporarily—until this other demand is relieved.

This is a vitally important concept: When another stress becomes greater than the pressure of alcohol, an alcoholic will quit drinking. He will be doing so against his will, but he will stop.

Families, friends, and counselors of drinkers need to understand that stress is an ally; yet many try to shield the alcoholic from tension and problems and are fearful that anxieties and difficulties will make him drink more.

In many cases that is exactly what happens; but the alcoholic may reach a point where some outside force becomes greater than the pressure of alcohol and he will stop drinking. The stoppage may be temporary; he may "fall off the wagon," but some day, as with me, it may become permanent.

Each time I swore off the bottle it was because I was pressured by my circumstances. The first time I quit was because of social pressure. I knew I was making a public spectacle of myself and I wanted to prove to everyone that I was not a drunk.

Then I quit to save my marriage. I knew if I didn't do something about my personal appearance and stop being an absentee wife and mother, that Jon would leave me. I realized this one night when we went to a party and I got so polluted that he completely ignored me and spent most of the evening talking to a very sober, well-built, pretty brunette.

Always before he had tried to keep tabs on me, supervising my every move. I was really scared when it dawned on me that he was not going to tolerate my drunken behavior any longer. So I quit. And I tried to stay sober, but it didn't last.

Next I quit because I couldn't afford to drink. I ran us to the brink of bankruptcy. There simply was not enough money for food and shelter, let alone booze. The few times I got drunk during this period was when I got "freebies" by bumming a bottle of wine from friends or neighbors to entertain a nonexistent dinner guest.

But the last time I quit—January, 1976—I did it for me; to rid myself of the revulsion I felt when I looked in the mirror. I hated myself so much I either had to change or die.

Actually, the first step toward sobriety when an alcoholic decides to quit is a fantasy, another *if only:* "*If only* I could stop drinking." No alcoholic, when he stops, thinks he is doing so forever. I always believed in the back of my mind that I would abstain long enough to get everyone off my back, long enough to overcome the stigma of being a drunk, and then I could start drinking again, but when I did I would be able to control my intake.

There isn't an alcoholic living who hasn't thought this way. We all tell ourselves that if we can stop long enough to gain control then we can eventually become "normal" drinkers.

It does not matter why an alcoholic stops drinking. His motives are irrelevant. All that matters is that when he quits, for whatever reasons, he does what is necessary to find his way back from alcoholism to sobriety so he won't start drinking again. Actually, there are four phases an alcoholic has to go through if he is going to achieve permanent sobriety, and abstinence from alcohol is only the first. The others are: selfishness, surrender, and serenity.

Phase One: Sobriety

I was a resident cynic, along with everyone who knew about my drinking, the last time I quit. I was like those of you who go on a diet every Monday to compensate for all the extra calories you consumed over the weekend. By mid-afternoon you have given in to the urge to eat a piece of chocolate cake for a snack. After you devour the cake you figure you blew the diet anyway, so you top things off with some ice cream. Then, at dinner you're so miserable because you cheated that you take two helpings of potatoes and gravy.

On and on it goes until next Monday when you start another diet. The only difference between you and me is that booze, not food, was my downfall.

I had stopped for short periods of time before, but since I had no foundational program to replace my drinking episodes, since I did not know *how* to quit, I couldn't resist the old routine for very long. Yet, the last time I stopped it was different for many reasons.

I was determined not to drink but decided that instead of stopping forever, which is a terribly long time, I was going to stay sober just for one day at a time. To hell with yesterday and tomorrow; all I wanted was to get through today.

Also, I was thinking differently. Some undefined, positive thing was happening. My mind was tuning in to the possibility of sobriety rather than the impossibility of overcoming addiction. And for the first time in my life, I was relying on God. I knew I could not save myself. I had already tried. So when I quit this last time, I asked God to save me from myself and the booze. He did. He gave me power that can come only from Him.

At the end of seven days I was feeling quite sanctimonious. I had gone 168 hours without a drink. Then I went two weeks, then three, then thirty days! I had remained sober for one full month and surprised even myself. Even then I can't say I believed I was going to succeed but I had some hope that this time I would win.

Phase Two: Selfishness

Self-preservation is the second phase of the initial recovery period. *If an alcoholic is going to stay sober he has to center completely on himself while he is withdrawing from alcohol.* Any emotional sidetracks will do him in. He has to focus solely on his problem because he cannot handle anything else.

Selfishness is an integral part of recovery. An alcoholic has to be so dedicated in his pursuit of sobriety that nothing else matters. We've been taught that selfishness is wrong, and certainly, doing what is detrimental to others to get your own way is morally wrong. But if an alcoholic is rehabilitated, everyone benefits; so the selfishness involved in recovery is essential, not harmful.

When an alcoholic is drinking he doesn't worry about what he does or whom he hurts; all he cares about is getting a drink. When an alcoholic is sobering up he *cannot* worry about what he does or whom he hurts. His drive to stay sober must be as strong as was his desire to drink. He cannot afford to let anyone or anything stand in his way.

If a man has to quit his job, or a woman has to leave her family and go somewhere for a few months until she gets her head together, so be it. If a father cannot cope with being around his children while he is drying out, then he may have to leave home until he is able to fulfill the father role. A person may have to terminate long-time friendships or even break ties with certain family members in order to stay sober. *Sobriety is worth any price that has to be paid to maintain it.*

Once I had been sober for a while, I was willing to do anything—within the bounds of reason—to stay that way. I was able to think more clearly because the booze was out of my system, so I could formulate plans and make decisions. I was determined to stay sober; nothing else mattered.

My first field of combat was with *my family.* I talked with them about what I was doing, knowing they felt it was a sham. I told them how I had set out on a course to freedom and I would not let anything or anyone keep me from reaching my goal. I informed them that they would have to take care of themselves and their problems for the next month or so; that I was going to be in limbo, available only to myself. I was going to see that Claire Costales stayed sober.

I knew if I was going to succeed that I had to seek after sobriety with as much zeal and vengeance as I had generated when I pursued drinking. I was intensely committed, twenty-four hours every day, never letting down my guard for a minute, consumed by the thought of not drinking. I wanted to stay sober so badly that nothing else mattered. I knew my husband and children would survive if I didn't cook their dinners or mop the floors, but if I failed, my drinking could destroy us all.

I told my family to pretend I'd died. (In a way, the old Claire had.) I said they'd have to depend on themselves and each other, but not on me. Although they wanted me sober, they didn't understand what I was going through and balked at my approach. So I had to be selfish enough to tell them that I didn't care if they were displeased, angry, or inconvenienced. They'd had all those emotions when I was drinking. Now they'd have to live without me for a while longer so I could overcome my addiction.

It wasn't easy for any of us. The changes in my personality were immediately visible and this forced a major adjustment for Jon and the children. They couldn't "use" me anymore. There were many times when out of guilt I'd said yes to the children when I should have said no. I was starting to feel better about myself and wouldn't tolerate the snappy, rude remarks I'd overlooked before. I was "sane" again and could respond in normal ways. Although they hated the way I had been they weren't sure they wanted the new me because they had to learn to live with a wife and mother who was sober and in control of herself. In some ways it is as hard for family members to cope with these changes as it is for the alcoholic to stop drinking.

Dr. Terry Davis, who heads an alcoholic rehabilitation program for women at UCLA, says that when an alcoholic starts to sober up he "makes dramatic changes, usually within a few days, but the family's not necessarily ready to change."

She also notes that children may initially resent their mother's sobriety because she wants to take back from them the responsibilities she had relinquished while she was drinking. A rehabilitated alcoholic herself, Dr. Davis shared, "My kids used to say, 'You were a lot more fun when you were drinking.' It was true. I didn't discipline them and I gave them things to make up for my guilt."[1]

I absolutely refused to let anyone or anything upset me. I set my mind on one thing: staying sober. I refused to get involved with anyone's problems. I rejected all negatives. I realized that this was my last chance, that I would have nothing or nobody unless I was selfish enough to keep away from the booze.

I remember one time my husband had a conflict with one of our daughters. Normally, I would have fallen into the old, established pattern and refereed the disagreement. But when they came to me I simply got up, went to my room, locked the door and refused to listen to either of them. They were astonished and for a while were so angry at me they forgot to be mad at each other.

Later, when they tried to drag me into the dispute I told them I had to expend all of my emotions only on myself. I was being selfish to be kind, and many positives came from such situations. Now Jon and the children have fewer conflicts because they've learned to be responsible for working out their own relationships instead of expecting me to act as a mediator and do it for them.

My second battle involved *my physical consideration*. Alcoholics are notorious for neglecting themselves. During those first few precarious weeks of sobriety, I had to learn to take proper physical and emotional care of myself. A fellow drinker, whom I met at an AA meeting (he was on his fifth time around, trying to conquer the bottle), shared a technique called HALT that had been extremely helpful to him. HALT is something many people practice as part of their daily living, but as a recovering alcoholic it was a revelation to me.

HALT is a simple pattern for living. It means Never get too HUNGRY, too ANGRY, too LONELY, or too TIRED. Those four things lower your resistance and make you more susceptible to booze or something else. I never saw that man again but I took his advice and still apply it every day of my life. I eat regularly and well. I control my temper and verbally vent my feelings. I turn to people for help and I get proper rest.

Phase Three: Surrender

It was Sunday morning. When I opened my eyes the first feelings I had were those of disgust for myself. I had gotten drunk again the night before. An instant feeling of panic gripped me because I couldn't remember what had happened. Where had I been? Who else was there? What happened to whom? Who caused it? (Probably me!) The bits and pieces I did recollect disgusted me even more. I remembered screaming into the telephone at someone, making slurred excuses for being drunk. I recalled that it had been raining. Raindrops splashed on the sidewalk and rushed through the gutters. I vaguely remembered running outside in my robe. Behind tightly closed eyelids I hoped I had dreamed it all.

I glanced at the newly decorated bedroom chair where I usually threw my robe at night. It was there, looking as if I'd rolled in the mud, as I very well might have. Oh God! I clasped my hand to my mouth, muting my shocked explanation. I hadn't dreamed it! It was real.

I closed my eyes once more and pretended to be asleep, hoping to avoid my husband's detailed account of the night before. I just didn't want to know any more about the fractured pieces of last evening. I wanted to go to sleep and never wake up. However, I was interrupted by the shrill ringing of the phone on my nightstand.

"Hello," I said sheepishly.

The soft voice at the other end of the line seemed strangely familiar, yet I couldn't connect it with a face. "How are you feeling this morning?" a female voice inquired politely.

Instantly, it all came flooding back into my memory. This was the voice of the person I had been screaming at on the phone last night. A familiar knot of guilt formed in the pit of my stomach. "I promised I would call you this morning. Do you remember?" she said.

"Oh, yes!" I lied, trying desperately to recall what she had said last night.

"It's quite normal not to remember. I've been there myself." Before I could respond she continued. "My name is Margaret and I'm an alcoholic."

I was disgusted and devastated. How had I come to this? "I'm not an alcoholic," I responded defensively. "I was just upset last night and had a little too much to drink. This has never happened to me before," I lied for a second time. "I'll be all right. Thank you for your concern."

"That's not what you told me last night," she persisted politely. "Last night you were concerned about your drinking and you begged me to help you," she said firmly, but not smugly. "That's the reason I called you this morning. And besides, you made a promise to me." I was mortified at having made such a fool of myself again. "How would you like to attend an A.A. meeting with me today?" she continued. "I'll be glad to come and get you. I can be there by 11:30. Okay?"

"Oh, thank you very much for asking me," I stammered, fumbling for words, "but I'm fine now. I'll have to go another time. I can't leave my children today."

"Come on now," she countered. "I'm sure your husband would be glad to watch them for an hour. I spoke with him briefly last night and he seemed like a reasonable man to me."

"I don't think so," I interrupted. "Maybe some other time." I was irritated by now.

"Well, at least let me give you the address in case you change your mind."

I tried to protest but she insisted that I write down the information and read it back to her. So I did, only to get her off my back.

"I know you're having a bad time now," she said.

"And I'll be praying for you. You might try praying for yourself. What have you got to lose?"

"I do. I pray all the time." I lied again.

"Well, take care of yourself. You know that God loves you even if you don't love yourself." And she was gone.

I hung up the phone and lay back on my pillow. My head was pounding with my usual hangover headache. Between waves of nausea my stomach felt like I'd been through major surgery. I was a total mess. I began to replay the telephone conversation in my head. "My name is Margaret and I'm an alcoholic." I couldn't understand how on earth the woman could say such a thing. Like it was something to be proud of. It disgusted me to know she was an alcoholic. It was beyond my comprehension why she would want to tell anyone about it.

"I see you're awake." Jon startled me as he appeared in the bedroom doorway. "Who was that on the phone?"

"It was a lady from Alcoholics Anonymous," I mumbled.

"What did she want?" he asked in a critical tone.

"She wants me to go to one of those meetings with her." Without waiting for his reaction, I blurted out, "Do *you* think I need A.A.?"

"I don't know what you need. All I know is that you need to stop drinking," he said angrily. "Do you know what you did last night? Do you have any idea?"

"Yes!" I screamed. "That's enough. I'm trying to do something about it. I'm going with that lady to an A.A. meeting today." Oops. I had said it now! Well, at least it would get my nagging husband off my back. And it would get me out of the house. Maybe I would just go shopping at the mall and pretend I went to A.A., I thought.

I jumped into the shower and let the warm water soothe my aching body. The shower temporarily relieved some of the symptoms of my hangover. After carefully selecting something to wear that would disguise my pasty, hungover look, I got dressed and joined the rest of the family at the breakfast table. Jon had prepared pancakes for himself and the three children, as he usually did when I was hung over, and the children were just finishing when I appeared. I think they were somewhat surprised to see me out of bed before noon.

"You look nice, Mommy," Dawn said, in her always optimistic eight-year-old voice. "Are you going somewhere?"

"Yes," I answered to my surprise. "Mommy's going to an A.A. meeting. I'm going to see if the people there can help me stop drinking." I was astonished to hear myself talk this way. I had never before acknowledged my problem, when I was in a sober state, to my children.

"I talked to a lady on the phone this morning. She said she had been just like me for a long time until she found A.A. and a power higher than her bottle. She was able to get help there. Maybe I will, too."

"I'm glad, Mom," Dawn said. "I know you'll be all right now and I'll be extra special good and I'll help you. We'll all help. Won't we?" She was looking for a spark of approval or enthusiasm from the rest of the family—her twin sister Deborah, brother Jon and her daddy—her eyes darting from one face to another, but nobody shared her optimism. They all looked so defeated I could hardly stand the feelings of guilt welling up inside me. They were more painful than any physical pain I have ever endured. I glanced at the clock. It was 11:15, so I excused myself and announced I was leaving. I started for the bedroom to get my coat and Jon followed me, closing the door behind him.

"You don't have to go to that A.A. place, do you? I'm sure you can stop by yourself if you really try." Then he hesitantly reached out to put his arms around me. "I love you. Isn't that enough? I'll try to help you."

"NO!" I screamed. Tears welled up in my eyes. "You don't understand. I can't stop on my own. I've tried, believe me. I've tried! You know that better than anyone. Please don't make this harder for me," I begged. "Just let me go and at least give it a chance."

I turned and walked out the front door, down the sidewalk, and got into my car. I checked to make sure I had the address, glanced briefly at the directions and started the engine. Suddenly I was determined to really do something about my problem, whatever it was called. I thought again about the phone call from Margaret and started crying. "God loves you," she had said.

"I hope so, I sure hope you do, God," I said aloud through my tears. "Please! Oh, please! Help me! I've tried everything and nobody or nothing seems to be able to help me. You are my last resort, God. Please help!"

By this time I was crying so hard I could hardly see the road. Suddenly, I felt a warm glow all through my body. I had an inner peace and serenity like I had never experienced before in my entire life. My body got warm from head to toe. I felt like a tiny infant nestled comfortably in her mother's arms. I was totally engulfed in a glorious, indescribable feeling of inner tranquility and love.

As nearly as I can estimate from my location on the freeway when I "came to," the sensation had lasted three or four minutes. To this day I have no idea how I managed to operate the car, but I'm quite sure that God had His hand on the wheel.

Now I was more determined than ever to get to the meeting. Instinctively, I knew that this was the moment. This time I knew I *could* and *would* make it. Nothing could stop me. I felt as if I had received, directly from my

Maker, a guarantee to succeed, a miracle I'm sure, and I have only become more certain of that fact as the years have passed.

Phase Four: Serenity

I had a difficult time trying to find the address Margaret had given me. Twice I took a wrong turn, but I wasn't about to give up. I pulled into a gas station and called Margaret from a phone booth. She told me how to get there.

A short time later I entered a large, overcrowded hall. "I'm so glad you decided to come," Margaret greeted me. I looked around the old, converted courthouse. Above the podium, where everyone could see it, was a large poster with the Serenity Prayer printed on it.

God, grant me the serenity to accept the things I cannot change, courage to change the things I can, and the wisdom to know the difference.

That prayer perfectly described what was in my heart.

I remember thinking to myself, no wonder all of these people are sober. They have all had the same kind of miracle I had. I looked around the room at them. They looked so much like me; nicely dressed, beautifully manicured ladies, men in expensive suits, young people in blue jeans and T-shirts. They certainly did not fit my definition of an "ALCOHOLIC."

I frequented that A.A. clubhouse every day for the next thirty days. I listened and learned from people who successfully conquered the bottle. I took note of all the different methods of staying sober. I tried everything. The things that worked for me I held on to and the things that didn't, I discarded. I trusted in God during the intensely bad times and He never let me down.

After I had been sober for a couple of months, as my thinking started to clear a bit, I realized there was something different about me; that I was, and am, physically and mentally different from "normal" folks, whatever that means. But I knew that an average, seemingly stable person was not like me. I had a different reaction to alcohol than most people. Alcohol had always given me a tremendously intoxicating high. It caused such euphoria that it was hard for me to imagine anyone not loving it. I was astonished to find out that non-alcoholics have a completely different reaction to alcohol. Drinking does not do for them what it did for me. They get to feeling quite dizzy and disoriented after only two or three drinks, and in fact, have full knowledge of how much liquor will make them sick or drunk. They know when to stop.

Not only did it not occur to me to stop after consuming a reasonable amount of alcohol but I don't remember having a choice. The only choice I had was whether or not to take the first drink. I learned at those meetings what it means to be an alcoholic.

How It Works

Repeating the Serenity Prayer helped me cope with daily living. I could get through the day without booze because I knew in my heart that my heavenly Father was going to pick me up no matter how many times I fell. I did not have to be afraid anymore of what I would say or do, or how people would respond to me, or of taking a drink. I simply "let go and let God," and went about the business of living.

Prayer works very simply. First, you call on God, taking the focus off yourself and putting it onto a Higher Power. Then you admit your inadequacy and His strength. Confess your weakness. Saying "grant me" means you are finally asking for God's help, admitting that you cannot do this alone. In the Serenity Prayer you are asking for serenity—the peace and freedom from the agitating craving that every alcoholic has. Serenity comes only when God grants it to you. Without Him you cannot make yourself or anyone else happy. The prayer deprograms you from going for a drink to going *toward* God, the Source of all peace.

I knew I was going to have to do a lot of hard work myself, but I wasn't alone anymore. I had asked God for help and He delivered a miracle. For ten years my husband had tried to get help for me, but to no avail. He had spent $72,000 in his efforts to rehabilitate me. I had been admitted to the mental ward two times, completely drunk on both occasions. Nobody there worried about my drinking or seemed to care why I had been admitted. And I was drugged the entire time I was confined. For an alcoholic, that's a legal binge.

Alcoholics do not belong in mental wards. They belong in rehabilitation centers that specialize in treating their disease. Rarely are they given medication unless it is during the detoxification process, and then only for a short time to prevent convulsions or D.T.'s. Not only was I readily given drugs when I was in the mental ward, my illness was not treated. I don't ever remember any of the nurses or doctors referring to the fact that I drank. The psychotherapy only stirred up guilt feelings and gave me no answers whatsoever. When I finally turned to God I felt like His answer was delivered in a split second.

I felt good for the first time in my life. In the past I had viewed people who talked about *the Lord* all the time as goodie-two-shoes or hypocrites. I'm sure there are people who look at me in the same light now. But it is impossible for me to deny the God who saved my miserable life.

I know that abstaining from alcohol was *my* responsibility as part of the recovery process, and I had to be wise. I decided to be good to myself. I took time making decisions. I tried not to make things too complicated or difficult for myself. (Most alcoholics are masters of confusion.) I tried not to be too hard on myself and I stopped being overly critical. I was kind to myself and allowed time for my recovery. I realized that healing is a slow process. I was considerate when I wasn't doing well. When I slipped in one area, I considered ways I was doing well in other areas.

I started to do things that were morally right. I had thought that morals were only for religious people but I found out that the moral lessons in the Bible made great psychological sense. I learned that the Bible was not a hellfire and brimstone threat but a practical message to live by. I was on my way back now.

Note
1. Beverly Beyette, "Alcoholic Women Get In-Home Help," *Los Angeles Times,* September 9, 1979, "View" section.

four
Changing Careers

I don't want to imply that overcoming alcoholism is as simple as saying a prayer. Recovery is a slow, painful, and sometimes discouraging process, and it is vitally important that you understand some of the physical and emotional pain that accompanies withdrawal from the addiction. Knowing these things will help you help the alcoholic, and, if you are an alcoholic, will assure you that you are not the only person who has faced such pain and suffering.

Physical Symptoms of Withdrawal
Pain and grief are extremely personal; each of us has a different level of tolerance to them. When I cut my finger or have a headache I may hurt twice as badly as you do. Or, depending on my maturity, stability, and what

the relationship was like, I may be able to accept and adjust to the death of a loved one better than you. So it is impossible to describe the hell of withdrawal in other than a subjective, personal way, although the physical symptoms will be essentially the same in all alcoholics. Unless you have gone through it you cannot relate totally to such pain. If you have ever quit smoking you might have a minor idea of the intensity. Part of my recovery treatment was writing poetry.

THE WAY BACK

Sweating pain was on my brow,
   my evil friend had got me now.
With heaving, gulping strangled pain,
   I fought and fought and fought again.
And still you haunt me every day,
   reminding me that I must pay.
If I'm to see a happy day,
   my evil friend please go away.
The remnants that you left behind
   are lost inside and hard to find.
And when one raises up its head,
   I fight until the damned thing's fled.
So keep them coming; I'll be strong,
   'cause I am bringing God along.
Now I'm the victor
   and you have to lose.
Between God and the bottle
   it's God that I choose.[1]

—Claire Costales

I will describe, as accurately as I can, the physical symptoms I suffered. I shook a lot, although it was not visibly noticeable; you would not have looked at me and said, "She's shaking," but my insides felt like I was walking on a vibrator. I couldn't pour a cup of coffee without slopping it all over.

I had chills, the kind you experience when you are coming down with a virus. My whole body was cold inside; I know now that was due to poor circulation. I was extremely nervous, chain smoking up to three packs of cigarettes a day. I have since learned smoking was my way of dulling the craving for alcohol in my system.

I had no appetite. I was nauseated intermittently for several weeks. I was so turned off to eating that I had no energy whatever for six weeks. My resistance was so low that I caught every bug that was going around during those first few months of withdrawal. I was plain old sick a lot of the time; sometimes sicker than I ever was with a hangover.

As the alcohol was released through my pores, I perspired so profusely that I had to bathe twice a day, but I still felt dirty. My body was cleansing itself from prolonged impurity. I also had agonizing aches and pains in my joints. I was more aware of these physical sensations as my dulled senses returned; so I hurt more instead of less as time passed. I realize now what a marvelous mechanism the human body is to have taken the punishment I thrust on it for fifteen years and, within a matter of weeks, to purify and begin to heal itself.

Emotional Symptoms of Withdrawal

During this time I was constantly fighting depression. The hardest emotional battle I faced was staying in good spirits despite the lousy way I felt physically. I would get bogged down when I started thinking what an awful person I was or that I was fooling myself—I couldn't really learn to live without booze. I was terrified of the unknown, of what life would be like and what demands would be made on me when I was sober. I knew how to be a drunk; I wasn't sure I could be anything else.

Mental attitudes are important during this time. Those who work or live with an alcoholic who is drying out must remember that encouragement is a primary recuperative factor during this portion of the recovery. Staying on top of things when you feel half dead and wish someone else could finish the job is exhausting. It took a sheer act of will many times to keep from giving in to my depression, chucking it all, and soothing myself with a bottle.

As I shared before, when I was confronted with emotional problems I handled them by writing them down. I expressed myself freely in words. Pencil and paper became my therapy. I ran for them when the going got rough.

I found another problem was that I could not concentrate. I thought in isolated facts rather than related concepts. I'd lose my train of thought, sometimes rambling as I talked. My mind was so saturated with alcohol that my thought processes were disrupted. I had to force myself to listen, to tune in, to pay attention to details. When I'd been drunk details hadn't mattered. Now they were stepping stones back to sanity.

Little everyday things loomed as great demands. I had to concentrate intensely on everything I did or I could not do it. After a person has a stroke and loses his power of speech, thought, memory, or movement, he needs therapy to retrain his thinking processes. I needed the same kind of help.

The most difficult emotional symptom of withdrawal I had to overcome was in the area of response. I was emotionally dead. I felt nothing. I had been a zombie in spirit for so long, tuned out to reality and on to booze, centered on that one consuming craving, that nothing else mattered. It was hard for me to respond to my children in positive, caring ways. I didn't want to be touched or imposed upon because I was afraid I would lose control again, but at the same time I was aware of their needs and sensed their love, which I had not done in a long time.

It was extremely difficult to be sexually responsive to my husband. I had broken the bonds of emotional contact and to have to resume, in full awareness of sensation, the most emotionally intimate relationship, was a frightening, offensive thing to me. It wasn't that I didn't love Jon, or that I didn't find him attractive; but I could not release myself to respond or initiate freely in such a close, threatening, give-take relationship. Yet, I desperately wanted to love and be loved. Rebuilding took a lot of time, patience and understanding. It was not easy for either of us.

Not too long ago I read a story in the newspaper about a girl who had been in a coma for over a year. The doctors were sure that she could not hear or respond, but her mother, with loving determination, visited her daily, talked to her, touched her, and after many months her daughter regained consciousness. In a way I was like that girl. I heard and saw the things that were happening around me and desperately needed to be loved, to be a part of life, but was unable to respond. Without the continuous caring and concern of my husband, family and friends, I could not have recovered. I would have remained in an alcoholic stupor for the rest of my life.

Implementing the Way

When I stopped drinking I wasn't satisfied with just being dry. I wanted quality sobriety. I didn't merely want to give up booze and crawl into a hole to hide for the rest of my life. I realized I had to rebuild my life piece by tedious piece. But how to start? I began with everyday things, not because they were easy for me to do but because they were necessities. They are things that will benefit the alcoholic, that will help him or her ease back into the family setting—such as doing dishes or laundry, reading the newspaper, pulling weeds or mowing the lawn. Simple, yet monumentally difficult tasks to the recovering alcoholic.

Friends and relatives can contribute to this part of the recovery by trusting him with responsibility and controlling his demands. They should make it as easy as possible for the alcoholic to perform by honoring his efforts and removing as many physical and emotional obstacles as they can.

There are certain regulations an alcoholic must follow if he is going to stay sober.

First, he has to *eat three meals a day,* like it or not. This isn't easy because the alcoholic is not accustomed to taking regular meals; sometimes he isn't eating at all. It is important that he eat at the same times every day, choosing nourishing food and a balanced diet, so that he can reprogram himself and avoid old habit patterns.

He must also *get the proper amount of rest.* Sleep is a big problem for the alcoholic because he has relied on chemical help for so long that sleeping without the aid of drugs—tranquilizers, sleeping pills, or alcohol—is extremely difficult. Some doctors prescribe medication for those who are coming off the bottle; but I am convinced that deprogramming is faster and more effective if it is done cold turkey. Taking pills may lead to exchanging one addiction for another. And, logically, using them as a crutch as only postponing the inevitable; he will eventually have to go to sleep without any artificial help.

Nights are lonely and difficult. Knowing that a counselor or friend is available, even at 4:00 A.M., will help the alcoholic get through the rough nights. There will be times when he does not sleep at all. Remembering that most people have sleepless nights and that such periods will soon subside keeps the insomnia in perspective.

Also, doing something—pacing the floor, reading, watching old movies on television—is better than lying in bed thinking and conjuring up a craving for a drink. Sometimes a warm bath is the answer, or a glass of warm milk. The recovering alcoholic should substitute any suitable thing for the sleeplessness and booze.

He should go to bed at a decent hour, usually not later than 11:00 P.M. and should try to sleep at least eight hours. By going to bed early he also establishes the pattern of rising early, whereas before he stayed up half the night and slept in during the day.

The recovering alcoholic is both physically and emotionally fragile during these early rehabilitative days so he should *take a short sabbatical from heavy work.* This is intrinsic to recovery. A drying-out drunk is so weak physically (many suffer from malnutrition) that he cannot do heavy labor anyway. Although this approach sounds as if it might disrupt the family's life, since most of the work we do is "minor" (how many of us clean the garage or rearrange the furniture very often?), it actually helps establish performance patterns.

The recovering alcoholic should plan to *get two to five hours of fresh air daily.* Being out-of-doors helps restore an alcoholic's general health and puts him back in touch with the physical world. Breathing clean air, feeling the sunshine or even the rain against his face, is a stark contrast to the unreality of the dingy bars and darkened rooms most problem drinkers frequent. Getting in touch with nature is an important step toward reality.

Before I was strong enough to go for walks, I would sit on the lawn, touch the grass and watch the bugs crawl. I'd lie on my back, look up at the sky, study cloud formations and watch the birds fly. Sometimes I went for long drives with all the windows open. Even cold or damp air feels good and helps the alcoholic regain his senses. As I improved I walked as much as I could without exhausting myself. The alcoholic should not do anything that will make him overtired, because fatigue makes him more susceptible to booze.

Another part of recovery is to *practice good grooming.* Many alcoholics are slovenly and unkempt. They don't care how they look or how their appearance or actions affect others. Good grooming, therefore, is another starting point. The drinker must once again learn how to take care of his body and his appearance.

When I was drinking I used make-up to disguise how bad I looked. I was pasty and grey and frequently disheveled. So, as part of implementing the way back to normalcy, I made a point of showering, fixing my hair, doing my make-up and putting on clean clothes every morning. I made sure I started the day right.

It wasn't long before I was more interested in how I looked. I started taking personal pride in my appearance and was pleased to see such a drastic change from the way I'd looked while I was drinking. My cheeks were rosy and the bags were gone from under my eyes. Taking care of my body was a way of making contact with myself, of reminding me who I was and what I was trying to accomplish.

A recovering alcoholic also has to *establish new social patterns.* Going places and doing things is important. When an alcoholic first stops drinking he wants to avoid contact with the world because he is afraid if he steps back into it he will start drinking again.

And if he isn't selective about where he goes and with whom, he just might. But socializing is an important step down the road to recovery. It offers an opportunity to rebuild neglected relationships and establish new ones.

I had only two rules about socializing. The first was, *do get out!* My husband and I started by going to a movie or on a walk. We went out to dinner, but only at places where alcohol wasn't served. (So we ate at McDonald's a lot. It didn't matter.) We took our family on picnics or camping and went to the park close to our home after dinner. We started doing things other families do.

The other rule was, *do not go into an alcoholic setting!* It is foolish for an alcoholic who is trying to stay dry to expose himself to booze. The world makes drinking look like such fun. It's friendly to have a beer with a buddy. It's romantic to linger over a glass of wine. It's relaxing to have a toddy when your nerves are frayed or if you've had a hard day at work. It's courteous to have a couple of drinks at a party. To me it was suicide; so for six months I didn't go near a place where alcohol was served.

I am amused and somewhat disgusted at an idea I've seen portrayed on television, in the movies, and perpetrated by well-meaning friends or acquaintances. For some reason, a lot of people believe that the way for an alcoholic to learn to handle his addiction is to expose himself to booze and resist the temptation to take a nip. In this fantasy his dramatic recovery occurs the instant he is offered a glass of vodka, or gin, or Scotch, or Bourbon, or anything else. He stares longingly at it for several minutes then triumphantly pushes it aside and is cured.

What a ludicrous idea! Life is not like that! Exposing an alcoholic to liquor during the early stages of recovery is like giving a withdrawing heroin addict a syringe, a spoon, and a fix.

Jon and I also turned down invitations we would normally have accepted just to be polite; we didn't go anywhere just because it was expected of us. We decided we would go somewhere only if we wanted to be with the people or because we could have fun. We avoided any situations we thought might cause me anxiety. We didn't offer explanations as to why we wouldn't come. We simply said no to anyone who could have possibly jeopardized my sobriety. That is part of the selfishness of recovery.

Learning How to Live Again

An alcoholic lives abnormally. His entire existence is centered around the bottle. In advanced stages of the disease he is drunk more often than he is sober. So when he stops drinking he has to learn how to live again. When I woke up from alcoholism after fifteen years, my emotional maturity was that of a seventeen-year-old girl. I had to start from that point of arrested development. Most of you know how hard it is to get back into a routine after you've been on a vacation. Think of how difficult the adjustment would be if you'd been gone for years rather than weeks or days. That's the kind of situation an alcoholic faces when he starts to sober up.

Because his drinking has been such an inconvenience and embarrassment to friends and family he may be expected to pick up the pieces of his fragmented life as if nothing had happened. That is not possible. The transition takes time. But there are some things the drinker can do to hasten the establishment of satisfactory behavior patterns and flow back into the mainstream of life.

One way I reeducated myself was by *observing "normal" people.* I watched how my neighbors managed their lives—what time they got up, what foods they fixed for meals, how they disciplined their children, when they cleaned house and shopped—all the general duties most women take for granted and do without thinking. In some cases I copied their behavior to the letter until I could establish a workable schedule of my own.

I quickly realized that I wasn't the only one in the family who had been living abnormally. Our household had no routine. The children came and went almost as they pleased. They did not help with any of the chores. After all, when I was drunk I didn't care if they made their beds or helped set the table. Much of the time I wasn't even home to fix dinner and was too hung over to worry about breakfast. So now, three children—Jon, age seven, and Deborah and Dawn, twins age nine—who had never known a nonalcoholic mother, had to learn a new life. I had to develop rules, standards, and regulations for all of us to follow. Suddenly it wasn't much fun having a sober mother. I was infringing on my family's freedom.

I demanded that the children clean their rooms before they left for school each morning. They had to do their homework before they could watch TV. I set up schedules for them to follow and expected them to help me with the housework. To my surprise, after a week or so they became accustomed to the new routine and stopped balking.

As I said before, I got up early, at first about 7:30 A.M. (And that almost killed me, because when I was drinking I stayed in bed until noon.) I would shower, dress, make the bed and prepare breakfast.

I know that to most of you that is so simple you cannot relate to how much turmoil it caused me. I felt as if I had climbed Mount Everest just getting through the first hour in the morning. It was a monumental task. I am stressing this so those of you who live with an alcoholic will understand how demanding even uncomplicated jobs can be when he or she is in this transitional stage.

After the children left for school I would have a cup of tea and rest for an hour or so. Sometimes I would listen to music or read. I was exhausted because I had to think about every move I made. It was like when you are learning to drive a car—nothing is automatic. You have to concentrate on every detail; put the key in the ignition; be sure the car is in the right gear; foot on clutch; foot on accelerator; foot on brake; signal left; signal right. Overwhelming!

About mid-morning I did a few more menial jobs around the house—a load of laundry, the breakfast dishes, dusting. And I always fixed myself a nutritious lunch and ate every bite of it. I didn't just grab a sandwich; I sat down and savored my food. That was my next rest period.

In the afternoon I went out. That was when I spent time in the out-of-doors. Sometimes I would visit friends, browse through stores, take a walk or a drive, but I always left the house. I stayed away until time for the children to come home from school. When they returned, we spent time together; something we had all sorely missed. We got to know each other for the first time.

I think I should mention that at first I did not grocery shop by myself. In California all supermarkets and corner stores have liquor departments. I was afraid I wouldn't be able to resist picking up a bottle so I didn't go alone. Foolish as it may sound, I was also embarrassed. I thought that the checkers at my local store where I had purchased many bottles of booze might notice that I had stopped buying, and that they would figure out I was an alcoholic because I had bought so much before and suddenly I wasn't buying any more.

Another thing I did was to *make a schedule.* I cannot stress enough the importance of establishing a routine. Dr. Joyce Brothers has observed, "Setting goals and pursuing them is a key to an alcoholic's recovery."[2] Families and counselors must be aware of the value of scheduling in the life of a recovering alcoholic. It is almost as if he makes a commitment to do certain things at specific times rather than to drink. Instead of thinking, "I must have a drink," he says, "I have to mow the lawn," or "I must read an article in the magazine," or "I will go for a walk."

Scheduling and setting goals are synonymous. When he is drinking, the alcoholic forsakes all of his goals and dreams. Once recovery begins he must have something to look forward to or he will dwell on the past and start drinking again. Rev. Pat Shaughnessy, pastor of Northwest Community Church in Phoenix, recently said that "the way to get rid of problems is not to dig back into the past but to look to the future and control it by setting goals and objectives." It is imperative that the alcoholic do this.

At first I tried to make sure I completed at least one task a day. That may sound like pittance but it was one more thing than I had been doing. Then as I felt better and gained more control, I added activities to the list. Of course, at first I tackled the "have to's" I had so severely neglected. I needed to start doing the hundreds of things associated with my roles of wife, mother, and homemaker. Eventually I worked out a schedule which I still follow closely.

Scheduling also helps the alcoholic avoid his usual drinking time. I was an afternoon nipper. Early each afternoon, after I had halfway done some household chores, I would sit down to relax and watch a soap opera. And, I'd have a drink. Then I would become so engrossed in the trials and traumas of the soap characters that I'd drink to drown their sorrow. In other words, I used afternoon television dramas to create a craving for alcohol. By the time I sat through three of them I was polluted. So, for me, it was especially important that I stay busy during that time of day. That's why, in my schedule, I left the house in the afternoon. I completely changed my setting.

That time of day was particularly hard for me. It was a time when I was alone and knew no one was there to stop me if I started to fall. If I couldn't get out in the afternoon I would make phone calls. I also asked people to phone me during those hours instead of disrupting my schedule by phoning when I was busy. I repeated the Serenity Prayer hundreds of times during those first crucial days. But I didn't drink.

Approaching the Disease

As time progressed, I started believing I could stay sober. But I had one other hurdle to overcome: I had to decide how to approach my disease. Obviously, I had faced the fact that I was an alcoholic; but until reality and reason overtook fear and fantasy I would not face the fact that I had an incurable, terminal illness. Gradually, I realized I had a fatal disease and that I had to approach my alcoholism in the same way I would if I had cancer, diabetes, or multiple sclerosis.

Alcoholics Anonymous teaches that we must let go and let God. We must live one day at a time. These are both good concepts and they helped me accept and adjust to the truth about my disease and to deal with it in a positive way. To control the symptoms I have to live on a maintenance program twenty-four hours a day. But I want to stress that does not mean I have to dwell constantly on the problem of alcoholism all of the time.

I will not live my life in reverse, dwelling on the past which cannot be affected or changed by anything I do. I had to decide to look forward to what can be rather than looking back on what was. So, although I have a terminal illness, I concentrate on the program rather than the problem. I live in a positive way, knowing I can control the progress of the disease and that I will stay in remission as long as I choose to do so. With God's help, every person who has been affected by alcoholism, either as a drinker or a victim of a drinker, can look forward and grow when these positive steps are implemented.

Notes
1. "The Way Back," by Claire Costales, © 1980.
2. Joyce Brothers, "Joan Kennedy's Road Back from Alcoholism," *Good Housekeeping,* April, 1979, p. 114.

five
Cravings, Crutches and Weaning

I'm sure most of you have settled down in your favorite chair to watch a television program or read a book and have been hit with an incessant desire for a piece of chocolate cake, a dish of popcorn, or something equally delectable. You aren't hungry—after all, you just finished dinner an hour ago—but you have an appetite for the taste of a certain thing. You *crave* it.

Alcoholics also have cravings but their cravings are not the same as I describe above. An alcoholic does not drink because he wants to *taste* liquor or because he has an urge to sample it for its flavor. Some of us get so desperate we feel like drinking anything or taking any substance, such as pills or cough syrup or cheap wine or rotgut whiskey. In a moment of desperation, whatever is around will do. Cooking wine, though not very tasty, works fine in an emergency.

An alcoholic doesn't think about how good a glass of Bourbon or fine wine would taste the way you think about how good a cup of coffee would taste. The drink-er's craving for alcohol is different from an average person's appetite because it is grounded in addiction to a chemical substance. Deprogramming requires a basic understanding of what cravings are and how an alcoholic uses them. What is a craving?

A craving is a mental obsession coupled with a physical need. The alcoholic's physical need is his addiction to booze. He is hooked on it as surely as the drug addict is hooked on cocaine or heroin. His body demands it.

The mental obsession is that he is totally convinced that he cannot live without alcohol. Whatever situation he is in, he is certain he cannot alleviate or handle it without a drink. He is emotionally dependent on the drug.

Creating Cravings

An alcoholic has to have a reason for drinking, so he creates cravings. He believes people will think he is insane because he drinks so much. So in order to justify his consumption he creates a problem to be upset about, and by manipulating circumstances he fabricates a visible excuse for drinking. He then has a logical explanation for why he is drinking himself to death. By doing this, he doesn't appear to be crazy. Usually he is not aware of what he is doing; he is motivated subconsciously by his addiction.

Let me explain how a problem drinker creates a craving, using an example from my own life. One morning my husband asked me if I would do laundry because he was low on underwear. It was not an order; he asked very politely and it was a reasonable request. But by 2:00 that afternoon I was in a rage. What nerve! Asking me to do laundry when I was staying sober just to please him.

Consequently, I decided I'd show Jon. I'd take a drink so he would see what his unreasonable demands did to me. It was his fault I fell off the wagon and I believed I was perfectly justified in drinking because of the way my husband had treated me.

That's a created craving, a setup. I used Jon's normal request to camouflage my addiction. Many times I provoked fights with either my husband or my children because if we had a disagreement I could blame them when I drank.

Since cravings are uniquely intrinsic to the individual drinker and his or her situation, they come in diverse forms and are hard to label. There are, however, some general behavior patterns that are recognizable as created cravings.

Depression is one form of created craving. When the alcoholic goes into a depression for no apparent reason, it is a setup for drinking. He will become melancholy, start feeling sorry for himself, and hit the bottle.

A created craving might come in the form of *anxiety*. The alcoholic contrives something to worry or be fearful about. He makes himself nervous and uptight so he can take a drink to soothe his nerves.

Belligerence is another type of created craving. The drinker finds things to pick on, disagree with, or become agitated about. Then he drinks to subdue his anger and calm his spirit.

Another less obvious type of created craving is *manipulation*. The alcoholic subtly twists facts and circumstances so he can drink. A man I know who was trying to dry out started running regularly as part of his recovery process. One day the sole came loose on his tennis shoe so he asked his wife to take it to be repaired, which she did. Then, because his shoe was in the repair shop and he could not run he started drinking again. He blamed his wife because she hadn't demanded that the shoe be fixed when she took it in instead of leaving it overnight. He made her his scapegoat.

How to Identify a Craving

When the alcoholic starts his sobriety program his greatest worry is that he will drink again. He thinks he cannot control the urge to drink; that is because he does not recognize the cravings he creates. The depression, anger, frustrations, self-pity, and fear he experiences are all forms of cravings. But to him they are feelings he's always had; ones that led him to drink. So, a vital step toward recovery is identifying his cravings so that the alcoholic can nip them in the bud and act contrary to them. He must be able to isolate them and call them by name.

Behavioral scientists believe that the most intense physiological cravings occur intermittently and then last for only a few seconds. When an alcoholic creates a craving, his body signals his brain that it is physically in need of alcohol. His brain then responds by saying, "Yes, you do need a drink," thereby contriving a mental obsession.

Once the drinker learns to identify his cravings he can deprogram himself by sending a different message to his brain when the need for alcohol arises. Instead of transmitting, "I need a drink," he can send, "I need to talk to a friend," or "take a walk," or "I don't need a drink, I just think I do." When the alcoholic isolates and labels cravings he is then capable of resisting them at the physical level; then the mental obsession will disappear.

Again, in identifying cravings, I can only tell you what

worked for me. First, I had to *understand and sort out my feelings.* Many times I was fearful but acted angry, so I assumed I was mad about something. Or I'd be defensive when I was feeling vulnerable. As I started drying out I examined every feeling I experienced before I acted on it. In many ways I was emotionally dead, so I had to identify *what* I was feeling. I labeled it, called it by name. I found I had been misnaming many of my emotions.

Next, I had to *decide if the feeling was legitimate or if it was a craving.* In other words, did I actually have a reason to be upset, angry, or disturbed or was I contriving a situation?

I remember an instance after I had been dry for several days when my daughter was giving me a hard time because I wouldn't let her go somewhere. She reminded me that when I was drinking I was a nicer mother because I let her go places and do things.

Her remark allowed me to use her normal, childish reaction to create a craving. I needed a drink so badly so I told her, "Okay, you want a drunk for a mother, you can have one." I sent her next door to get a bottle of wine from the neighbors. She was demoralized that I made her go and guilt-ridden that she had thrown me back into my drinking patterns.

Subconsciously, that was exactly what I wanted. I wanted to be able to blame her for my falling off the wagon, to make it her fault. But when she brought me the bottle and I tasted that drink, suddenly I knew I had forced a craving. For the first time I had successfully identified a setup. I immediately stopped, threw out the rest of the booze and told my daughter what I had done. That was the last time I ever trapped myself into taking a drink. I realized what cravings are and started watching for them.

Identifying a craving is no simple matter. At first I suspected every feeling was a craving. This was not negative, just necessary. It put me in touch with my emotions. Gradually, I was able to spot a craving without scrutinizing everything I felt or did. As I said before, each alcoholic has his or her own unique cravings. He cannot start deprogramming until he understands what they are and how he creates them.

I found it was helpful for me to *list my cravings on paper.* I kept a daily account. By doing this I was able to determine the time of day when I most needed a drink, what behavior patterns I used as a reason for drinking, and toward whom I directed them. Keeping this diary made me face my mental obsession toward alcohol. When the alcoholic begins to recognize nervousness, anger, frustration—or whatever his created problem is— as a craving, he is well on his way back.

Family, friends or a counselor can help in this area. Even if a problem drinker is not trying to sober up, those around him can point out his created cravings if they are aware of them. For example, when I drank because Jon asked me to do the laundry, he could have honestly said, "You are not drinking because I asked you to do the laundry. You are drinking because you had to have that drink and the laundry was a good excuse to hang it on."

DO NOT LET AN ALCOHOLIC USE YOU! Don't be a scapegoat. You can't stop what he is thinking but you can state the truth as you see it. Look for cravings and label them for him until he is capable of doing this for himself.

Weaning the Alcoholic
Deprogramming from alcohol is a slow process. Recovery from any major illness takes time, and healing

from alcoholism is no different. As cliché as it sounds, time is a great healer and gradually eases the pain that is caused by the loss of alcohol. The longer a drinker goes without booze the less he has to have it. Although the acute physical craving subsides in about thirty days, mental dependency lingers for months, and in some ways for a lifetime. Tests prove that traces of alcohol are still found in his system up to two years after an alcoholic stops drinking. That is why a recovering drinker dare not ever take so much as a sip of liquor.

Recently information has surfaced about studies which theorize that social drinking is possible for alcoholics after their treatment. All of our research, however, proves that the outcome of such theories is disastrous.

Actually, deprogramming from alcohol is much like weaning a baby and is most effective when it is done with the least amount of discomfort. If a child is thoughtfully and lovingly separated from his bottle, then he benefits. If not, if that physical and emotional appendage is removed carelessly, without feeling or concern for the pain and confusion the baby is suffering, weaning can be destructively traumatic.

To eliminate the trauma of withdrawal when she weans her child from the breast or bottle, a smart mother will substitute something positive for what's being taken away. She teaches her infant to drink from a cup, gives him a cookie or graham cracker to nibble, reads him a story or takes him for a walk when he starts whining for his bottle. She supplies acceptable crutches to compensate for his loss.

Just so, an alcoholic needs crutches to help him start walking the path back from alcoholism to reality. He needs things to lean on for support during those first difficult days of sobriety.

For some reason which I have never been able to

understand, we talk about crutches as if they were bad; but I have never heard anyone with a broken leg call them bad or unnecessary. We have been brainwashed into thinking that unless we can stalwartly stand alone, unaided by anything, and single-handedly battle any odds, that we are less than mentally healthy. Yet, you and I both know that all human beings need help in getting through certain phases of our lives.

Dr. William Glasser says that using replacement crutches is "positive addiction." In his book by that title he says, "I believe there are a number of addictions that are good. I call them positive addictions because they strengthen us and make our lives more satisfying. They exist in sharp contrast to the common or negative addictions like alcohol or heroin, which always weaken and often destroy us."[1]

Positive addictions are good crutches and, as an alcoholic, I know I need them to stay sane and sober. I cannot walk healthy and whole through life without them any more than a one-legged man can walk without crutches or a prosthesis. However, not all crutches are good! Some are negative crutches.

Any mind-altering drug is a negative crutch and should be avoided at all costs! Some alcoholics delude themselves into thinking that if they drink only beer or wine they can sober up. Not so. Beer and wine have alcohol in them just as hard liquor does. Other alcoholics substitute, frequently with the help of a well-meaning but naive doctor, other drugs such as tranquilizers or uppers and downers.

Let me explain why it is better to stop drinking cold turkey. When you substitute other drugs for alcohol you are still catering to a physical addiction. As soon as the drugs are discontinued you have to learn to live without them. Since many of them are habit-forming, all you are doing is replacing one physical addiction with another. I am convinced that is one reason why there is such a widespread epidemic of poly-drug abuse in this country. Too many doctors are prescribing too many drugs to too many alcoholics.

I tried using pills several times because I was looking for an easy way out. When I was taking the medication I still didn't have control of my life. The pills alleviated my physical discomfort caused by the withdrawal from alcohol but I merely went from one fool's paradise to another.

I ended up running from doctor to doctor, describing every symptom I could think of so I could get prescriptions for more pills; I lied and fooled the doctors. There is no way a doctor can know you are an alcoholic unless he sees you drunk repeatedly or you tell him the truth about your condition. But the medication did not work. Ultimately, I found that there is no easy way out, only the right way. Negative crutches don't work; they only make you more dependent.

A positive crutch is any acceptable substitute for alcohol. Some that settled the physical craving for me are candy, gum, tea, soda pop, sugar, or fruit. Sugar helps the cravings most because a severe blood sugar imbalance occurs when an alcoholic stops drinking. I carried candy and gum with me everywhere I went. (Life Savers really were a life saver.) I always had fresh fruit of some kind in the house. Hot drinks helped too, especially tea loaded with milk and sugar. I found that soda pop or fruit juice pacified my desire for cold liquids.

These foods and beverages are not taken in the place of regular meals but as substitutes for booze any time a physical craving strikes. As the addiction subsides, so will the need to lean on these crutches. But until then, better a candy bar than a cocktail, or a glass of tomato juice than a Bloody Mary. Not only must the physical desire be satisfied but the mental obsession for alcohol must also be dealt with. I discovered several psychological crutches that I still lean on very heavily.

Life's simple pleasures help to ease the intensity of psychological addiction. I had been drunk so often for so long I had forgotten how to relax and enjoy life. I had to slow down, pay attention to details, and take pleasure from the everyday activities I had ignored and neglected for so many years. I had to learn how to "stop and smell the roses" and savor the goodness of life.

For example, if I was going to bake a cake I'd read dozens of recipes and select just the perfect one. No more packaged mixes or bakery cakes for me. Then I would spend a lot of time preparing and icing it. I didn't just throw it together, I savored the experience.

A gentleman I know returned to a pre-drinking hobby, woodworking, and is now earning his living custom-making plaques and picture frames. A lady returned to a pastime she had sorely neglected—reading mysteries. She told me that anytime she had a craving she ran for Agatha Christie or Alfred Hitchcock. She didn't merely read. She concentrated on the way the authors structured the language, looked up definitions of words she did not know, and ended up taking some literature courses at a local college. Savoring the simple pleasures of life is a wonderful crutch.

Physical activity eases the physical as well as psychological addiction. Walking, running, jogging, tennis, golf, swimming, weeding, mowing the lawn, mopping the floor, exercising—anything that helps channel energy, build vitality and strength, and is physically constructive—is vital. Most alcoholics are so out of condition that they desperately need to participate in some kind of fitness program, but they should ease into it.

Substituting mild, physical activity for a drink is a good way to begin.

For instance, when I would get to the point where I thought I could not resist the urge to take a drink, instead of heading for the bar I'd head out the door for a brisk walk. To keep my mind off the booze I had to concentrate on what I was doing. I counted the steps I took, looked at leaves and bugs on the ground, counted the cracks in the sidewalk and walked, walked, walked until the urge subsided.

People are another, and probably the most important rehabilitative crutch. An alcoholic has fractured, if not destroyed, many interpersonal relationships so he must build new ones and reestablish those that are salvageable. But that is easier said than done because he has forgotten how to be a friend or build a friendship.

I was almost paranoid when I first sobered up. I thought everyone was watching me, knew I was a drunk, and was condemning me and eagerly waiting for me to fall off the wagon. So it was very difficult for me to say even as much as a hello to a neighbor or the clerk at the supermarket. I, as have all alcoholics, had become so insensitive to others, living in my alcohol-sodden world, that I did not remember how to live in a social setting. A vital part of my recovery was building personal relationships with people, believing I could enlist them and rely on them when I needed assistance.

I had to step out on faith. I had to learn to trust my family, friends, and even strangers; to confide in them and discuss my feelings and frustrations; to reveal my fears and fantasies rather than run to the bottle.

As I made contact with the family of man I gradually regained some self-confidence. I started doing helpful things for people, like driving a neighbor to the doctor, doing her hair or nails, baking cookies for the local school open house, or running an errand for a friend. As I did these things I related to the needs of others rather than to my own.

The most vital "crutch" on which I lean is my trust in God. All other crutches have to be undergirded by His strength and His love. I don't dare face any day before committing it into God's care.

Each morning, before I do anything—even if it means getting up before anyone else does—I spend at least twenty minutes in prayer. I go over everything I have to do during the day, anticipating how I will handle each activity or task. I take inventory of the people I may meet, the problems, trials, temptations, frustrations, barriers—anything that may interfere with my goals for the day—and commit them all to God. Then during the day, whenever I feel insecure or inadequate to face a situation, I remind myself and God that I don't have to do it alone; He will help me.

Then every evening, our whole family sits down for thirty minutes of Bible reading. We don't do anything except read the Bible, learning about God and His people. When my children were preparing for their first communion we read about the first Lord's Supper, seeking its purpose and meaning for our lives.

I don't ever go out to speak to any group or sit down to work on a book without giving everything over to God in Christ's name.

By taking advantage of all these crutches, the days become brighter, the cravings less intense and more obvious. I have once again begun to learn to walk through life. What a joy it is to return to the land of the living from the place of the dead!

START WITH TODAY

Crawl in the bottle and stay there said she,
   there's no other place left to go.
You have made it your life,
   and it's all of your strife—
It's to you both your friend and your foe.
But what will you do when the liquid runs out?
It will happen my friend—of that there's no
doubt.
Where will you go and what will you do
   when what's left is the empty bottle and you?

Please help me sweet Jesus, she pleads in the
night
With a last breath of hope in this terrible fight.
I've been everywhere and no one could see
   what that demon rum had been doing to me.
But somebody told me that you have the key
   to enter my sick-darkened heart.
So, if you can do it—
   I'll work my way through it.
My trouble is: Where do I start?

You start with today, and you hope and you pray,
   and you stay close to God as you can.
You never forget the sweet Lord you met,
   that's when your real life began.[2]

                  —Claire Costales

Notes
1. William Glasser, *Positive Addiction* (New York: Harper and Row Publishers, 1976), pp. 1,2.
2. "Start with Today," by Claire Costales, © 1980.

six
Building Self-Esteem

As an alcoholic I had a very low opinion of myself, and with good reason. I had disgraced and embarrassed myself and my family, stifled my creativity, and wasted my potential. I had failed as a wife and mother and, most importantly, I had not lived up to my own expectations and desires. I don't know if I drank because I had a poor self-image or acquired a poor self-image because I drank. I only know that when I stopped drinking I was faced with the task of undoing what I had been and what I had told myself I was.

Any recovering alcoholic has to face the reality of who and what he is and has become. But he cannot pull himself out of the gutter unless he starts programming some positives into his self-concept. How can he do this? How does an adult who has openly and flagrantly destroyed himself put the pieces of his battered life back together? How can he learn to like and accept himself?

Get to Know God

The first step in building a proper sense of self-esteem rests not with the drinker but with his Maker. I've already told how I was at the end of my rope and it was only when I cried out to God, as I then perceived Him, that I was finally able to stop drinking. I have talked to hundreds of alcoholics and each has acknowledged that without a Higher Power he could not have stopped.

I did not think of God when I was soused, but many times after a binge I begged Him to help me get out of the mess I'd gotten myself into and promised I would never drink again. I did, of course, but I know now that even then I had a glimmer of faith left. It was only after I had exhausted every human resource to no avail that I selfishly decided I truly had nothing to lose by trusting God. I turned to Him when I had no alternatives left, yet He received me with open arms. *That* is love!

Trusting God was the best thing I have ever done. He does for you what no human can. He is totally faithful and always there; so when I let myself down or others fail me, I still have Him. Instead of turning to the bottle for consolation I can turn to my Lord. Now, when I am upset, frustrated, or battling a craving I turn to God.

There is still much I do not know about God, but I am learning; and I find that the more I learn about Him the better I understand and accept myself. He shields me from myself and the bottle.

In this area, I think it is important to interject the fact that many alcoholics I interviewed, who have successful sobriety, admitted to me that they weren't certain at first that it was God who helped them. However, they also admitted that further down the road they realized that, although they had no conscious knowledge of the fact, it was God who was responsible for their recovery. I have never met anyone who is healthfully recovered—not just dry but who has quality sobriety—who is an atheist. I have never met anybody who has recovered who doesn't have some belief in God. For some, it is a very basic belief that there is a God and that being moral and good and kind is the way to live. Generally, they have an innocent cleanliness about their faith. Others just believe wholeheartedly in a higher power.

I must say for myself, even though I knew it was God who touched me in the beginning, I believed it was impossible to know Him without being a learned Bible student. I was wrong. At this point I know much more *about* the Lord than I did when I started; however I honestly don't think my *faith* has changed in any way. I have always believed in the existence of God. I do say, though, that the messages of the Bible have become practical guidelines to better pathways for my life. I found this kind of attitude to be common among alcoholics who are recovered.

Get to Know Yourself and Others

One of the reasons I started drinking was because I didn't know myself. I didn't know why I wanted to drink, what booze could do to someone with my personality, or what my weaknesses and strengths were. I did not know Claire Costales, so I couldn't relate to or help her. I could identify only with her roles, what was expected of her, and what she was supposed to do.

As an alcoholic emerges from the insanity of drinking, he is faced with the effects of what he has done, and unless he gets a firm grasp on who he is he is likely to start drinking again to hide from the horror of the past. He must get acquainted with himself. I used the following simple steps to gain the basic self-knowledge I so obviously lacked and needed.

I started by *being a friend to myself,* treating myself as I know I should treat my friends and as I wanted other people to treat me. I talked to myself. Instead of letting ugly, unrealistic thoughts run around in my head, I would tell myself how happy I was going to be now that I had stopped drinking. I would say, "Claire, you are strong and you can do anything you set your mind to."

I would scold myself when I put myself down in any way and would praise myself, out loud, for the things I was accomplishing. "Hey, good girl, Claire, congratulations. You made it through the day without taking a drink. You really know what you're doing with your life. You're in charge of it now." Things like that.

I'd look at myself in the mirror for at least a few minutes every day and pick out physical attributes I liked about the way I looked. I studied my facial features, the way I stood and sat, my profile, my body build. I discovered that I frowned a lot, so I practiced smiling until it was as natural as scowling. I related to myself as a person. Perhaps to some of you, studying yourself in the mirror sounds like an egotistical thing to do, but for me it was awakening a reality that I was a real, live human being who walked, talked, breathed and had some things going for her.

I praised myself consistently for conquering the bottle. I thanked God for giving me the strength to resist temptation. The fact that I was staying sober was a miracle and I patted myself on the back for my contribution to the effort. It must have been good input because I made it all the way back.

To my amazement, people started treating me the way I was treating myself. They smiled at me and laughed at witty remarks I made rather than my drunken stumblings and ramblings. They looked up to me (all five feet of me!) rather than down on me as I learned to stand straight and tall and think more highly of myself. Seeing the dramatic changes that resulted from my new attitude motivated me to try even harder.

I also had to learn how to *be a friend to others*. During my drinking years I was emotionally divorced from family and friends. I hadn't wanted to hear what they had to tell me. As I was recovering I realized that friends are an external support system and are essential to both physical and psychological health.

I started relating to others by talking with and listening to my family. There is no way I can describe the joy I experienced when I introduced the "new" me to friends and relatives and started rebuilding those relationships. Discovering that my children were exciting, vital people whose ideas and opinions could stimulate me intellectually was an ultimate blessing. I was contributing to their lives, and they were responding to me!

I realized I needed at least one close friend, a confidant. (Incidentally, I still do. It is imperative that I have one person outside the family to confide in and dump on.) I prayed and asked the Lord to send me someone I could love and trust, someone He could use to help me. I was fortunate. He gave me Kathleen. She knew about my problem and what I was trying to do with my life and was willing to be my friend. Our relationship has been a satisfying experience for both of us.

In building this friendship, I knew if my self-esteem was going to grow that it could not be one where Kathleen did all the giving and I did all the taking. I wanted a reciprocal relationship, with neither of us imposing in any way on the other, but contributing as needs arose. When Kathleen describes what happened as we were "growing together" she says she learned a lot about herself as she watched me go through my struggles. Although I knew I could call her any time, for any reason, I took a step toward maturity by considering her feelings and schedule and phoned or visited her only when it was reasonable.

In the early weeks, as I was drying out and developing my program—using myself as a guinea pig—I had a rough time. I spent many nights talking to Kathleen on the phone, or she would come over and keep me company. I was afraid to leave the house for fear I would end up in a bar. We would talk, drink cup after cup of tea, and sometimes just sit without saying a word. I needed human contact to keep my head above water.

I learned something else about myself during those times of inspection and introspection. I had wanted to be popular so badly that I had spent my life acting on the assumption that the more people I knew and the more friends I had, the more I was accepted. That was a lie.

I know now that it is the quality of a relationship and not how many acquaintances I have that matters. So now, instead of responding to anyone who happens into my life, I have had to set standards for relationships. I want to contribute and be liked but I do not want to be used.

I felt so lousy about myself for so long that I had forgotten how to be me. I so desperately wanted to be accepted and appreciated that I let people use me for a doormat. I let them walk on me. In my sick mind I had decided that if someone did not criticize my drinking, they were my friend, so they could make outlandish demands on me and get me to commit myself to doing almost anything with no regard as to how it would affect me, my family, or my self-respect. If someone wanted money, I gave them money, whether I was donating our rent money or a quarter for a phone call. If they feigned approval, I did what they asked.

I don't mean to imply that everyone I had contact with treated me shabbily; there are a lot of good guys out there who don't use people. But a drunk is an easy mark. In defense of those who did abuse me, I must admit that they couldn't have done so if I hadn't let them. And I don't let them anymore; I had to before, to keep them from calling me a drunk. I don't worry about that now. I may be an alcoholic but I am one who hasn't had a drink for more than seven years now and who is liking herself better every day.

I also had to learn to *avoid people who affect me negatively*. An average person will automatically stay away from someone who degrades him. But I had done just the opposite because, when I was drinking, I wanted to be with people who brought me down so I could use them to create cravings and make them my excuse for drinking. Now if certain people are not good for me I refuse to have anything to do with them. I will not let them hurt me nor will I expose myself to them.

Since I've gotten to know myself I realize that criticism, even when it is offered lovingly by a friend, is extremely hard for me to handle. When it comes from an acquaintance or other less intimate party, and is unwarranted or unsolicited, I can choose to reject it. I do not have room in my mind for the kind of negative input strangers or mere acquaintances have to offer. Neither do I have the emotional stamina to handle what their remarks or opinions might do to me.

Let me give you an example. Suppose Harry, who lives across the street, says something to me like, "Oh, are you on the wagon again? How long has it been this time?" There was a time when a remark like that would have eaten at me until I'd have taken a drink to soothe my reaction. Now I wouldn't let Harry's remark take up one precious moment of my life. I have already paid my dues.

Let's look at what Harry said and why it can get to someone who is drying out. First, he asked if I was on the wagon again. That hits the nerve that reminds me I failed in the past when I tried to stop. The rest of his jibe was, "How long has it been this time?" implying that I can't really stop drinking forever. Harry doesn't have faith in me and his two short, jabbing sentences will shake my faith in myself if I let them. What he believes about me might easily make me feel like all of my effort is in vain, that I might as well take that drink and get the inevitable over with.

Let me tell you: IT DOES NOT MATTER IF HARRY HAS FAITH IN ME! Harry's faith in me, if he had any, would not change anything. Would his belief make a difference in the quality of my sobriety? No, it would not. After all, who is Harry? What is he to me? I probably won't remember his name a few years down the road and the fact that he is deviously reminding me of my past failures means he may be feeding some neurosis of his own.

This is how I handle the Harrys of the world: (1) I weigh their right to evaluate me—they have none; (2) I ask why they are evaluating me—their motives are suspect; (3) I decide how I should react—common sense dictates that I must dismiss their judgmental opinions.

I know when I was drunk I said some ghastly things to people, but I was not responsible for how they took them. Just so, Harry is not responsible for my getting upset over an inconsiderate, stupid remark he made. Harry is not going to be hurt if I get drunk because I let his insensitivity upset me. If anything, Harry will be boasting about how right his prediction was.

THE HARRYS OF THE WORLD DO NOT MATTER. An alcoholic has to willfully choose to disregard them and build relationships that can count for something.

Build for the Future

Not only did I need to get to know God, myself, and others, I also needed to set a few simple goals for the future. Obviously, my first one was to stop drinking. I have a fatal illness but it is treatable and can be brought into remission. I knew if I did certain things, which I have suggested in this book, I could prolong my life. So my primary objective was sobriety. I also wanted to repair and improve my marriage, which had suffered greatly because of my alcoholism.

I had some positive goals like getting the right amount of sleep, exercise, and food, and building constructive relationships. There were also negative goals, such as I would not drink, go certain places, think certain thoughts, or start something I did not intend to finish. I defined the goals, decided on specific things I had to do or not do to help me reach them, then concentrated on carrying through.

In the instance of my marriage, I decided I had to keep the house in reasonable order, be physically presentable at all times, and share all of my thoughts and feelings with Jon. I also had to listen to him when he communicated with me. I told him I was going to make a conscious effort to do these things and asked for his support. Although he was skeptical at first, I knew there was a better chance of getting his help if I asked for it.

I set one goal that those closest to me thought was unrealistic, actually a sort of fantasy: I was going to write a book. I was determined that the hell I had gone through was not going to be wasted; that if it was possible, others would learn from my mistakes. My father-in-law told Jo Berry how he and Jon's mother used to smile and nod when I would mention the book I was writing. They thought it was just another pie-in-the-sky scheme.

They had good reason to doubt me. I was a master at starting things and never finishing them. As you can see, I have changed. When I determine to do something, I do it. You are reading that book.

In rebuilding my life there were definite steps I had to take.

When I got to know myself, I reasoned that *I would have to change what I did not like.* Once I quit drinking I saw many characteristics that I wanted to modify or eliminate in my personality and character. I didn't like being a drunk. When I was drinking I thought of myself as a drunk, so I rationalized that I had a reason to slop around, not take care of myself physically, and mess up my life in general.

I look at myself differently now. I am an alcoholic but I am no longer a drunk; so I dress properly, watch what I say and do, and live according to the rules. I am always pleased when I share with people about my past and they are shocked that I am an alcoholic. They are surprised because I do not look like their mental picture of a drinker.

I had always thought I was not very smart. The truth of the matter was that I was not educated. I had chosen to remain ignorant and believe what other people told me instead of searching out facts for myself. I wanted to change that, so I started reading, listening to conversations, and collecting information about different topics. I started forming my own opinions. I know a lot more than I used to about almost everything. I like that about myself.

I was not physically attractive, at least not in my own

eyes. So, as I have already shared, I took a long look at myself, then I worked on grooming, choosing the right wardrobe, and presenting myself in the most positive way possible. As I changed my attitude about my physical appearance, and started taking pride in the way I looked and acted, I actually started liking myself.

I had spent a lifetime believing I had nothing to offer in relationships. As the youngest in a family of ten children I spent many years being pushed to the end of the line; so even when I was being accepted I was convinced that I was being rejected.

Now I think in terms of what I can contribute to a relationship that no one else can. I look for voids to fill that would remain empty if I weren't there. I have seen that I can help people and contribute to their well-being. As a result, I am offering something. I always could have, but I was looking at what I wasn't getting instead of what I could be giving.

As I changed what I did not like, *I had to build on what I did like.* It was difficult for me when I first stopped drinking to think of any positives about myself. But I forced myself to write down the things I liked, or at least one time had admired about myself. I could only think of three at first: I am loyal, extroverted, and articulate. So that was where I started. I realized that I had those few things going for me and determined to use them to the fullest.

I incorporated these traits into my goals. I decided that since I am articulate, I would share with anyone who would listen about my recovery from alcoholism. I wanted to praise God for what He had done for me. I am extroverted and enjoy being around people, and I certainly know my topic. Since loyalty and commitment go hand in hand, I have religiously pursued that initial goal of sharing my life and now have opportunities to speak in schools, hospitals, on television and radio, and at seminars. Everyone can find character traits with which to rebuild his life.

As I grew in knowledge and understanding of myself, I realized *I had to release what I had been and done* if I was going to feel permanently better about myself. That was no easy job. Intellectually I accepted that the past was over and done with, but emotionally I was hanging onto it. Ralph Waldo Emerson said that "most of the shadows of life are caused by standing in our own sunshine." That's what I was doing. I had to get out of the way, to let go. It was over if I would let it be.

When someone dies, after a very brief period of time we bury him, then no matter how difficult it is we go on living without that person. I knew if I was going to become a whole person I had to get rid of my debilitating habits and thoughts and eradicate my negative emotions. I had to lay them to rest.

I was told by Alcoholics Anonymous to look over the wreckage of my past. I had already spent ten years and thousands of dollars on therapists examining in detail the mess I had made of my life. I was literally buried in guilt and failure. I could not stand to look at the past any longer.

I realized that if I was going to make it I had to look ahead, pretend the past did not exist and not let anyone or anything make me look back. I didn't delude myself that it had not happened but I dwelt on the wonderful truth that, because I had joined to God through Christ, "I am a new creation; the old has gone, the new has come" (see 2 Cor. 5:17). Jesus did not make me go back and try to repair or rebuild the wreckage of my life—He accepted me where I was, without my doing anything except to turn to Him.

My formula for letting go consists of four simple

steps: releasing negatives, rechanneling thoughts, replacing bad habits, and remembering who and what I am.

Release Negatives

Release means letting go of things that are bothersome to you; things that make you feel hurt, fearful, or angry; things that detract from your joy and pleasures. One of my biggest problems was nurturing negative input. I would see or hear one little negative and I would plant it in my mind, fertilize it by dwelling on it, and water it to full bloom with my imagination. With that kind of attention, the negatives rapidly grew to huge proportions. I was a master at making mountains out of molehills.

So I had to release those negatives. To do that I had to label them as honestly as I could, then dump one whenever it appeared. Sometimes I had to resist the same thing dozens of times before I was completely rid of it.

For example, when I would start thinking about how badly a relative was treating me, rather than dwelling on that, I would release that negative and think instead about how wonderful my husband is to me, how sweet, loving, and patient he has been to me through all the times of trouble and trial.

Let me tell you what I have discovered: dwelling on negatives can kill your soul but dwelling on positives brings life.

Rechannel Thoughts

During the initial recovery phase many bad memories and experiences will haunt the alcoholic. His mind will need a "spring cleaning." I realized that storing up the bad and negative things took up space in my brain, thereby reducing its capacity for positive input. Since we only get out of our minds what we put into them, I found I could increase the quality of my life by adding positives.

First of all, rechanneling my thoughts meant turning off my head to everything connected with booze and filling that space in my mind with something else. Instead of thinking about what I had done, I thought about what I can do. The Apostle Paul instructs us to think about "whatever is true, whatever is noble, whatever is right, whatever is pure, whatever is lovely, whatever is admirable—if anything is excellent or praiseworthy—think about such things" (Phil. 4:8).

What an exciting concept! Thinking about excellent things! So, instead of drinking for entertainment or relaxation, I concentrated on praiseworthy things. I read and wrote and that helped curb the cravings; but there were still times when a craving came. When it did, I would do something nice for myself, like soak in a hot bath, fix my hair a new way, get a pedicure, or shop for a new dress. Eventually, through a constant rechanneling of thoughts, an alcoholic automatically does something other than take a drink.

I found it helped if I would say aloud what I was thinking and verbally admit that it was a negative thought. For instance, when I would get a craving and want to take a drink, I'd say, "The grocery clerk snapped at me and because of that I think she doesn't like me and I want to take a drink to soothe my pride. That is a negative thought and will hurt, not help me." I would say it repeatedly until I realized how ridiculous the idea was.

Reading good literature (the Psalms are especially uplifting) or listening to good music also acts as a catharsis to negative input. So does talking to someone, not necessarily about your negative thoughts but about something constructive instead. And, as you know by now, I recommend writing. Sometimes when I was overwhelmed by depressive thoughts I would write them on paper. I found that after about half a page I'd run out of downbeat things to say, then I could think about positives.

Replace Bad Habits

Habits are learned behavior patterns and, although it is not easy, they can be unlearned. An alcoholic has many horrendous habits to undo in addition to his addiction to liquor, which is a compulsive, uncontrollable habit. When I stopped drinking I knew if I was going to stay sober I had to revise my life-style or I would never conquer the bottle, because I was saturated with bad habits that contributed to my problem.

Just as I could not bear to look into the wreckage of my past, neither could I face the idea of changing all of those habits. So, instead of pessimistically dwelling on what was wrong with me and how to change my unsatisfactory behavior, I optimistically planned how to replace those detrimental habits with beneficial ones.

Let me stress: *I did not try to get rid of my bad habits.* Instead, I cultivated new, acceptable ones. I found that the bad ones disappeared as I established better ones. Replacement is the key to this reconstruction. Habits are learned responses and I found I could pick up a good habit as easily as I could a bad one. Since it is healthier and psychologically easier to actively do something than it is to try not to do it, I made a list of habits I wanted to acquire instead of the ones I wanted to get rid of. Then I concentrated on doing them rather than on not doing the ones I wanted to drop. It worked.

Remember Who and What You Are

The final step in letting go is based on remembering who and what you are. I am Claire Costales and I am an alcoholic. I will never be able to take another drink of liquor as long as I live. I have made a decision to live without it. I now am as committed to staying sober as I used to be committed to drinking.

There was a time when I could not admit I had a drinking problem. I was ashamed and pretended nothing was wrong, so I could not change. Now I realistically remember who and what I am. I am not embarrassed anymore to tell people about my illness. There was a time when I was and when I worked very hard at trying to convince everybody I could quit.

There was a difference in me this last time I stopped. In the past I needed people to believe in me. I wanted them to say, "We know you can stop drinking." This time, because I knew who I was and what I am, I did not need that assurance. I needed only to trust myself and my Lord. This time *I knew* I could do it, and that was all that mattered because I am the only one who can keep me sober.

I don't shy away from the topic as I once did. I refer to my alcoholism as an addiction and as a disease, and when I talk about it I also talk about my recovery. I use the proper terms so as to rid myself of the negative stigmatism that goes with the illness. I am comfortable using words like alcoholic, craving, disease, addiction, withdrawal, and drunk. I know myself, I like myself, I accept myself enough to live soberly with myself now, and I am growing every day.

seven
Call for Help

One of the most frustrating feelings we ever experience is that of helplessness. All of us have been in situations where we have desperately wanted to assist a person in need or to alleviate the suffering of a loved one. The families, friends, and associates of alcoholics usually are impotent when it comes to easing the mental and physical anguish of the problem drinker. They feel totally helpless, incapacitated by their own deep personal pain and their inability to be objective.

The drinker is also frustrated by his failure to stop drinking. He knows he *needs* to give up booze. He knows he *should,* that he is destroying himself and the people he loves. He *wants* to stop; he does not want to be drunk. But he does not know *how* to stop, and those who are closest to him and love him the most don't know how to help him forsake the bottle.

The simple fact is that *alcoholics need to be taught how to stop drinking!* When I decided to quit I knew I would need help to do it. I tried several traditional programs but none of them contained that vital "how." I kept expecting someone to give me instructions, to offer some procedure I could follow—to hand me a prescription I could use for permanently drying out, but no one did.

I read the material I got from Alcoholics Anonymous. The people who were quoted in the book said AA had saved them but they didn't say how. I needed a step-by-step directional program. In those days if I was going to buy more than one item from the supermarket I had to make a written list. My thought processes were completely fragmented. I needed someone to tell me when to get up, when to start breakfast, when to shop, when to bathe, when to go to bed. I was not capable of formulating a solution to my problem.

As time passed I realized that the more traditional approaches for combating alcoholism would not work for me. I tried AA, hospitals, doctors, clinics, even suicide. When I fell off the wagon I was so angry I wanted to lash out at all the people who were supposed to have the answers because they were not able to keep me sober. I tried to kill myself for the same reason. *I* couldn't keep me sober.

Finally a glimmer of hope surfaced. Despite all the failures, I still had a consuming desire to quit drinking. I knew I had a choice. If I sought God's help, put my trust in Him, and kept experimenting I knew I would find the way back. I was determined to build on the one positive I saw; my faith.

At least I was sure of what did not work. For the first time in years I started looking forward, anticipating rather than dreading the future. I knew I was going to succeed.

Find Someone to Help You

The key to my recovery, the "how" to stop drinking, developed when I got so desperate that I decided I had to ask someone for help. I didn't need an organization, a psychiatrist, psychologist, or a doctor, but another human being who would reach out to me, lend a hand and help me put together the bits and pieces of my alcohol-sodden existence.

I turned to a woman who had licked the same problem I was facing—a recovered alcoholic. This one-on-one, person-to-person relationship was the basis for my recovery, as it can be for any alcoholic who truly wants to stop.

If you are an alcoholic, I do not know what circumstances will bring you to the point of return, to the place where you want to not drink more than you need to drink. But I do know that *you can learn not to drink!*

If you are going to stop you must call for help. You might be surprised how much help you will get if you only ask for it. After I realized how desperately I needed a friend to be my counselor, mentor, and guide, I did the only thing I could think of to do. I made a list of all the people I knew whom I thought might help me.

I automatically excluded my husband and relatives because they had been so negatively affected by my alcoholism that they needed help themselves. Besides, I could not share with them what they had done to contribute to my problem.

Dr. Terry Davis, director of UCLA Extension's in-home help project for recovering women alcoholics and their families, and herself an alcoholic, says, "Alcoholism is a family process. The others in the family have to learn to cope because they have been focusing on the drinking person as the cause of their problems."[1]

She observes that the alcoholic family have stopped communicating and have isolated themselves. "They get locked into this little world where they're all sort of feeding off each others' illnesses," and she notes that they are themselves apt to have psychosomatic and psychological problems.[2] So at this early stage of recovery, family members cannot lend a helping hand.

In my list of people who might help me I had ninety-three names. Then I experienced a rude awakening: As I mentally sorted through the names I realized that out of all those friends and acquaintances there were only two I could turn to for the kind of committed help I needed. Of those two, one rejected my plea. I thank God the other one did not; but if she had, I would have kept on hunting because I knew a one-on-one relationship was the answer to my agony.

When you call for help you must promise yourself that you will not stop until you find it. If one person refuses, ask another. Look at it this way: if your best friend was lying at your feet dying and asked you to call for help, you would call until someone came to save him or her. I ask you to be your own best friend. If you are an alcoholic you have a terminal disease. It does not matter if the persons you ask to help you can't or won't—don't worry about what they say or think. All that matters is that you find someone to go through this with you. Your life depends on it.

Use the One-on-One Recovery System
The method I am sharing saved my life. There are several reasons why it is successful.

The first is that *it is a God-ordained method.* I did not know this when I first began the program, because at that time I did not know much about the Lord or the Bible. But as I studied and grew spiritually, I found that one-on-one assistance and training of one individual by another—what Christian teachers call discipleship—is God's way of saving, teaching, leading, reaching, and restoring people.

True discipleship is one person giving to another, devoting his time and talent to edify another human being, just as Jesus did with the twelve men He called to be His intimate disciples. For three years He worked with them intimately, investing time, prayer and tears in their lives. One of them betrayed Him but the other eleven founded the early church.

Jesus Christ always centered on the individual. Frequently in the Gospels we read that He had great compassion for people. He was sensitive and caring and always took time to help someone who was in need. If this one-on-one method worked for Him then it certainly should work for us.

Another reason the one-on-one recovery system is successful is that *it is flexible and individualized*. I developed the program by putting together workable bits and pieces from different sources. But I wasn't tied to a specific discipline, so the program includes things that helped me as an individual, not things that are required.

Primarily, it is successful because it stems from a basic need and meets that need. For me, the one-on-one relationship was what was missing in all other approaches. If an alcoholic is going to learn how to stop drinking then he or she must have a teacher who will share in that educational process. The one-on-one system supplies that teacher.

Still another reason for success is that the one-on-one program is based on the simple reality that *there is nothing anyone can do to change the past.* The only thing you can do about the past is forsake it. I did not want to go back, I wanted to move forward into a new life. I had to learn to forgive and accept myself before I could repair or make amends for the past. The alcoholic is encouraged to deal only with the present and gear toward the future. Concentrating on what is and what can be, rather than on what was, eliminates unhealthy guilt rather than stirring up old resentments and feelings. This method creates positives in relationships by giving the alcoholic something he desperately needs: hope for today and tomorrow. As he changes, people respond favorably to his new life-style and wounds are healed.

Most conventional methods burden the alcoholic unnecessarily by telling him he has to clear away the wreckage of his past. That's like telling a surgical patient that he has to perform his own operation. The thought of facing all the people I had hurt or embarrassed frightened and humiliated me beyond measure. I wanted to edify, not debase myself.

Also, I had no idea how far back in the past I should start clearing the wreckage. I had left a wide path of destruction throughout my fifteen years of alcoholism. I did not know where or how to begin remedying my mistakes. I couldn't cope with the idea of retreating to where I had been—dwelling on my failures and reliving some of the worst mistakes of my life. Many alcoholics tell me they have reacted the way I did.

Using this one-on-one system I found I could concentrate on the here and now. The past was over and was of no benefit to me other than what I had personally learned from it. I tried to project six months or a year into the future and visualize what it was going to be like to live like a normal human being. I thought about how nice life would be when people began to realize I wasn't the drunk I used to be. I could almost taste the pride of being able to say, "It's been a year since I've had a drink."

I wasn't certain that would ever happen, but I hoped and believed it would. Thank God, I don't need to project anymore. Knowing I'm in control of myself is the best high I ever had. Being drunk never made me feel this good!

Because the one-on-one system deals with the basic problem of booze and not with the results of drinking, it *takes a participant beyond physical dependence to sobriety.* The alcoholic uses his helper as a crutch until he can stand alone. He has someone to help him go another five minutes without a drink. He has someone to whom he is accountable, someone to keep him zeroed in on the one thing he wants to accomplish. He has *someone.*

In my program, it doesn't matter what a person has done before, who he has hurt or how low he has stooped. More than one morning I woke up not knowing where I was or what had happened the night before. I've demoralized my husband in front of his family and friends. I've neglected my children. But my gut instinct verified that if I was going to change all of that I had to care more about overcoming my addiction than I did about how lousy I was. As I prayed, I had the assurance that God had forgiven everything I was aware I had done, and all that was left was a disease that had to be treated. And God was able to help me here also.

Follow the Seven Steps to Deprogramming

People learn in different ways. That's why a good teacher will use various methods with his students. The same principle applies to alcoholics who are learning how to stop drinking. The one-on-one recovery system is a general approach, but within its framework, depro-gramming techniques will differ. There are, however, certain basic elements in the learning process that must be incorporated into any deprogramming efforts.

1. The alcoholic must verbally admit he is mentally and physically dependent on alcohol.

2. He must commit himself to abstain from drinking for a specific period of time, whether it is three hours or three months.

3. He has to decide what things he will do instead of drinking. He must plan substitute activities so when he has an urge to drink he can physically react by doing something else.

4. He must set aside at least one-half hour each day for meditation and self-evaluation. It is important for the alcoholic to be aware of the passing of old habits and to give himself positive strokes by implementing new, positive behavior patterns. With daily inventory the reinforcement is twofold. By writing down these new, positive changes the alcoholic reinforces his belief in himself and his ability to turn negatives into positives.

5. He must promise to take proper physical care of himself by getting the right kind of food, rest, and exercise. Alcoholics usually suffer from malnutrition, or at least from vitamin deficiencies. Booze isn't nutritious, but it does contain about seventy calories per ounce. So when a person is drinking, he doesn't eat properly. If he has been an addict for a long time he may have severe damage to the pancreas, gastrointestinal tract, and liver.

Proper nutrition is essential if an alcoholic is going to recover and regain his health. A high-protein diet is best because it reduces his desire for alcohol and also helps regenerate tissue that has been destroyed by the liquor. Alcoholics are frequently anemic and are also highly susceptible to respiratory infections. The iron and vitamins A, B, and C in a balanced diet will cure those conditions. At first, the drinker may have to take a vitamin/mineral supplement until his appetite increases and his resistance is built up.

6. He must stay as far away as possible from the temptation of booze. He cannot associate with his drinking buddies or go where liquor is sold or served without danger of falling.

7. As the initial step, he has to ask someone for help. He has to find a counselor/friend who will guide him through the first stages of withdrawal. He needs to be discipled by someone who cares.

In the next chapter we will discuss how a counselor/friend can help the alcoholic on his way back.

Notes
1. Beverly Beyette, "Alcoholic Women Get In-Home Help," *Los Angeles Times,* September 9, 1979, "View" section.
2. Ibid.

eight
Step by Step: Staying Dry

Let me introduce you to two people. Although their names have been changed they are real people who have been through this program. One is Angie. She is fifty-six and has been an alcoholic for thirty-three years. Now she has been dry for more than two years.

The other is Murray. He is thirty-five and has been drinking heavily since his teens. A year ago he was so desperate he asked Jon and me to help him with some personal problems, all of which were symptoms of his alcoholism. When he came to us he was not ready to admit he had a drinking problem, or that his life was messed up because of his drinking.

When I challenged him with the fact that he is an alcoholic he got extremely angry and rejected the idea. But after I took him through the procedure in this chapter, he not only acknowledged that he is a sick man but he has been dry for several months and is presently counseling an alcoholic friend of his. Angie and Murray both learned how to not drink.

Stimulate Pressure

There are two basic steps in the initial deprogramming of any alcoholic: getting him to stop drinking and helping him overcome the mental and physical dependency related to his addiction. The accepted school of thought is that until an alcoholic asks for help and wants to quit drinking there is nothing anyone can do to make him stop. That is not true. AN ALCOHOLIC DOES NOT HAVE TO WANT TO STOP DRINKING OR EVEN HAVE TO ADMIT HE IS AN ALCOHOLIC IN ORDER TO STOP!

Remember what I said in chapter 3? The alcoholic only seeks to relieve the pressure of alcohol when another pressure becomes greater. Since the alcoholic will not purposely introduce such a pressure, it either occurs accidentally, by an act of fate, through God's providence, or from someone else bringing it into the drinker's life.

In her book, Betty Ford says, "The thinking used to be that a chemically addicted person . . . had to decide *he* wanted to get well, before he could begin to recover, but it's now been demonstrated that a sick person's family, along with others significant and important to the patient can intervene to help him despite himself."[1]

If you know an alcoholic, chances are that you can get him to commit himself to stop drinking for a limited period of time. Usually, that is all it takes, because after someone has been sober for a month he is sane enough to realize he *does* have a drinking problem and he feels well enough that he wants to continue living without alcohol's insidious influence.

That is why I will go to any reasonable length to meet with someone who is a problem drinker. Of course, initially each alcoholic vehemently denies that he or she is an alcoholic. And I cannot convince them that they are any more than I can prove to you that God exists, but I can persuade them to prove to themselves that they aren't.

When talking with an alcoholic you can convince him that he might have a problem, or make him angry enough to prove to you that he isn't an alcoholic by talking about the problem and asking certain pertinent questions. As you approach the drinker, do not worry about his reaction or about offending him. At first he will be both defensive and frightened and will probably lash out at anyone who confronts him.

Betty Ford's reaction, when her family confronted her, was a typical one. She was shocked, did not remember much of what was said, was terribly hurt, reduced to tears, and resisted any suggestion that she was an alcoholic. *Then,* after a period of a few days, she realized they were right, had her welfare in mind, and consented to get help.

The following guidelines will help you help the alcoholic.

1. Discuss his problems and make him admit that in the past many of his miseries have been alcohol related. When I met Murray he was having marital difficulties which stemmed from his boozing, but he blamed his wife, complaining that she was always nagging him about every little thing he did.

When I asked him why she was always on his back, he said it was because he seldom got home from work in time for dinner. He said he was usually a "little" late because after a hard day at the office he liked to stop on the way home for a drink. When I quizzed him about what time he did get home, he confessed that many times it was 10:00 P.M. or later.

When I suggested that four hours was a long time for one drink, he admitted he never had just one and often had so many that he lost count. Finally, he reluctantly told me he knew his wife nagged him because he consistently came home drunk late at night. That admission was his first step on the way back.

2. Ask him if he has memory lapses or blackouts. These are a common symptom of alcoholism. If he does, you might ask if he has seen a doctor, since such drastic physical problems are normally related to stroke or brain tumors and certainly would alarm an average person, sending him scurrying to the doctor for a diagnosis. If the alcoholic is ignoring such severe symptoms it must be because he knows their source but is unwilling to admit the cause.

3. Discuss how alcohol affects his behavior. Most people who drink socially, even if they get drunk once in a while, aren't identified as drunks. Ask the drinker to evaluate his drinking behavior for you. When he drinks, does he act erratically and stand out in the crowd either because he gets loud and obnoxious or because he silently melts into a puddle of booze? Do his speech patterns change? Does he have what could be termed "drinking bouts" where he acts contrary to his usual personality and character? Is he oblivious to what is happening around him, unstimulated by his environment? If so, alcohol is doing some very negative things to him and he should be astute enough to see that.

4. Discuss when, where, what, and how often he drinks, exploring the fact that if he is an alcoholic there will be a pattern to his consumption. I have already shared that I drank in the afternoon when I watched soap operas. Another lady I know had a nip with her morning coffee for a pick-me-up, then nipped off and on all day, every day, until she was quietly and pleasantly drunk by bedtime. She never sat down and drank just to drink. She did with alcohol what a nibbler does with food. She picked at it, consuming a little bit each time. That was her pattern.

Joan Kennedy was a sporadic drinker. She would go for days, sometimes weeks, without a drink. She usually drank after a period of stress. She would hold together until the crisis subsided, then hit the bottle. She did this when her son had his leg amputated, and frequently after she gave musical performances or had been involved in a demanding schedule because of her husband's political position.[2]

Betty Ford admits that she had difficulty accepting the fact that she was an alcoholic because she drank only when it was socially acceptable and never got sloppy drunk. But, in her social circles, alcohol consumption was almost always permissible.

In retrospect, she mused, "I think of the endless toasts at political parties, I think of the European trip ... and sipping booze out of paper cups, the liquor mixed with melted snow we'd scooped up off the windowsill of our train compartment: how romantic it seemed."[3]

I think of a famous movie star who is known for his inordinate consumption of beer, yet who marvelously avoids a pot belly and who never gets obnoxiously drunk. I dare not use his name but he is an alcoholic. He jokes that he has to have his beer, and his friends and fans see it as a cute habit and are amazed at his capacity for booze, since he drinks all day long.

The point is that alcohol consumption patterns are as varied and unique as each individual drinker. All alcoholics do not drink all day, every day, nor do they act the same way when they are drunk.

5. Ask the person what he does when he is faced with a problem. Have him outline for you, blow by blow, each step he takes in facing difficulties. One of them will be taking a drink to calm his nerves. He will invariably, at some point, retreat to the bottle when the going gets rough. He may not always get drunk but he will always drink when trouble is brewing.

6. Appeal to his common sense. Tell him that a person with any intelligence and self-respect will value his life enough to devote thirty days to evaluating the possibility that he may have a drinking problem.

7. Ask the person if he would be willing to help you if you were in the position he is in now. His response will give you some idea of how badly he wants help. A quick yes usually indicates a receptive attitude and is his way of asking for assistance.

If he is not convinced by this time that he is addicted to alcohol then he has joined the ranks of the untouchables, at least for the time being; but chances are he will be responsive at this point.

Many people do not ask for the help they need because of misguided, foolish pride, but if they are given an opportunity to try something and save face at the same time they will do it. I think that is one reason this approach has been so successful. An alcoholic can accept your challenge and at the same time maintain his dignity. If he refuses your offer of help, at least your conversation has confirmed to him that he has a problem and he may respond later.

Begin the Way Back

Now, if the alcoholic says, "Okay, I'll quit for a month," then what do you do? There is no way a problem drinker can go without booze for thirty days unless he is led moment by moment through the first stages of withdrawal and is then nursed through the next few weeks. The procedure in the following pages is the ideal approach and is the most effective way to start deprogramming. Therefore, I suggest that if it is at all possible, the counselor/friend should strictly adhere to it.

When an alcoholic calls for help he needs a positive response. He isn't looking for a professional counselor; he is searching for a friend. Human qualities such as patience, persistence, empathy and concern are what matters. His counselor/friend has to be strong enough to teach the alcoholic how to live without booze and sensitive enough not to let him depend on him for sobriety.

Since it is important that the counselor understand the problem as thoroughly as the alcoholic does, he needs to know as much as possible about the disease. That is why alcoholics who are in remission make ideal counselors, they've been through it; but anyone who is willing to devote time and energy building a one-on-one relationship can become a good counselor. Most of the information a "helping hand" needs is found in this book and the basic steps a counselor should follow are listed and discussed in detail.

1. **After a person has thoughtfully and prayerfully committed himself to helping an alcoholic, the first thing he should do is contact the alcoholic's family.** The counselor needs to solicit their cooperation, explain in detail what's going to happen, what they might expect in the way of reactions in themselves and their loved one, and what will be required of them.

He must try to prepare them for their own new feelings. Although families support the concept of reforming an alcoholic, they experience mixed emotions as the drinker starts to change. Some are afraid of what the nonalcoholic will be like. Others resent the fact that their routine is being disrupted. No matter how bad the situation is, they may have grown comfortable with the problem.

Children who were doing poorly in school because Mom or Dad drank can no longer use that as an excuse for their bad grades. The wife who became a nag or let herself go physically because her husband was always loaded has to change her attitude and appearance. A husband who turned to the other woman or became a "workaholic" has to learn how to live with a sober wife.

When an alcoholic stops drinking, everyone's life is disrupted. Alcoholism is a family disease, and the entire family needs to get well, so the counselor should include them from the start.

2. Next, it is important for the counselor to contact the alcoholic's family physician. He probably has no idea that the patient you are calling to discuss is an alcoholic. I expertly hid my problem from my doctor. I attributed my hangover headaches to nerves and my shakiness and lack of appetite to a touchy stomach. My doctor saw that I was sick but he had no reason to suspect that the cause of my illness was alcohol. He did not know I drank.

A doctor has to rely on what a patient tells him, so a counselor should contact the doctor to inform him of the problem and to let him know what is being done. Every doctor I have talked with, as I have taken other alcoholics through my program, has been cooperative and supportive. Each appreciated being told that his patient was an alcoholic because it meant that the physical aspects of the disease could be properly treated.

Once the groundwork of family and medical cooperation has been laid, the actual therapy begins.

3. The counselor should take the alcoholic to a place where they can be alone, undisturbed for at least

five days. If you cannot afford to rent a hotel room, then perhaps you can arrange to use someone's cabin or similar hideaway. The alcoholic has to retreat from his normal surroundings, from the people and situations that are part of his drinking pattern. He must break contact with everything and everybody so he will be forced to face his drinking problem without input from anyone but his counselor.

THIS RETREAT PERIOD IS ESSENTIAL TO RECOVERY. During this time there must be no contact with family, friends, or acquaintances. No phone calls or mail. No visits from anyone. The alcoholic cannot be distracted by outside influences. The past has to be severed from the present.

4. During these crucial days the counselor's biggest job is to get the alcoholic to concentrate solely on himself and his disease. Because drinking is the core of his other problems, when he stops drinking a lot of alcohol-related difficulties will also disappear. He should not sidetrack onto any problems his alcoholism has caused but dwell only on his drinking problem.

The only way a counselor can teach someone to stop drinking is to get him to think only of himself and what he must do to control his addiction. The alcoholic cannot conquer his habit by being guilty about the past, by feeling sorry for himself or by drinking more. He must shut out everything and everyone and battle booze. Centering the person on self makes him face the basic problem. He cannot hide behind other issues. He is forced to constantly admit and deal with his cravings. He cannot blame others or his circumstances.

The counselor helps the alcoholic put everything in the background but the booze, and concentrate moment by moment on staying sober. During this process, the drinker is learning what he has to do to keep from drinking; he discovers how not to drink.

For these five days there is no room for anything else. The alcoholic must exclusively talk and think about staying sober, one minute, one hour, one day at a time. His "helping hand" is there to help him set goals and reach for them.

5. The drinker should never be left alone for those crucial first days. During this time the counselor needs an undying faith; he must convey his belief that the person he is helping will eventually stop drinking. As evidence of this faith, the counselor should let the alcoholic take his bottle with him if he wants, so he doesn't fear being cut off against his will.

The counselor should never lecture, but encourage his charge by telling him over and over and over that he can stop drinking. He should make him feel responsible so it will be hard for him to take a drink because he would betray the trust his friend has placed in him.

Until the alcoholic can function as an independent unit, the counselor acts as his alter-conscience, his encouragement, his hope for tomorrow. His "helping hand" is a passport to the way back. This unique relationship begins when the alcoholic calls for help and ends only when he can say, "I don't need you anymore."

There is no way anyone who has not suffered withdrawal can understand totally the physical pain involved. It is unrelenting, excruciating, consuming. The mental anguish is almost as intense, because the alcoholic knows he could relieve his misery if he took a drink. One precious jigger of booze and the hurt would stop.

6. As counselor and friend, you must identify with the person's suffering. This is hard for someone who has not been addicted. Here is one alcoholic's description of the pain of withdrawal: "My insides felt like they were tangled up together and would not work right. My head pounded, my joints ached, and I was deathly sick to my stomach. I couldn't sit, lie, or stand still because my body was crawling, vibrating, and thrashing; yet every movement I made hurt so bad that I cried from the pain.

"Moving felt like when I was little and had a compound fracture in my leg and they had to set it. And I wanted a drink so bad I was drooling and sweating. So much saliva actually rolled out of my mouth that I had to hold a washcloth over it. There were a few hours when I'd have killed for a drink. I mean that. If one of my own kids had been dangling a bottle of booze in front of my face I'd have murdered him to get it. I went to the medicine chest and hoped there would be a bottle of alcohol or Merthiolate there so I could drink that. It was hell."

7. **During this time, you must lend your emotional and physical support.** Touch the patient. Rub his shoulders, hold his hand, pace the floor with him, pray with and for him. Go through the ugliness at gut level as he experiences it. It isn't easy to be sympathetic to someone who, for the most part, has brought something so drastic and debilitating on himself. But you cannot play judge and jury. You must be a support system.

Accept the person as he is. Everyone needs approval; it keeps us going. Since an alcoholic has zero self-esteem, by accepting him you will help him accept himself. The alcoholic is paranoid during the first stages of withdrawal, so do not force him to do anything that is against his will, but take him as he is. That is one of the reasons I let him take his bottle when we retreat. He has to stop drinking of his own volition. I am not going to make him do it.

Do not reject any ideas or suggestions he makes, even when he rants, raves, and rambles. In the initial phase of withdrawal, he is much like a person who is coming out from under an anesthetic. He has been drugged senseless, and as he regains consciousness—as awareness returns—he will talk gibberish and nonsense. He will be weeding out many ridiculous notions and opinions. The whole idea of getting away is to let him reason himself into doing what is right and necessary.

Let him know you love him. Because of his actions and attitudes, the alcoholic is unlovely and unlovable. Yet, love is as necessary to him as booze or food. It's the one thing he cannot survive without, and paradoxically, the thing he denied himself as he drank.

Let him know you care. The fact that you are investing time and effort in his life speaks for itself, but he needs more than your presence, he has to hear you verbalize your care and concern.

Give him your undivided attention. Most alcoholics are painfully shy. Many of them start drinking so they can sum up the courage to face a group or participate in the everyday affairs of life. Up to this point, when the alcoholic craved attention, he drank. Like a child who misbehaves so he will be noticed, he used booze to draw attention to himself. So he needs your undivided attention as he is sobering up. The fewer interruptions there are the better it is for him. You should try to be his captive audience.

If you are going to counsel someone in this way you should make sure there are no loose ends in your life, because you will be unavailable for a minimum of seventy-two hours. The alcoholic has to see, from your example, how important this project is to you or you might lose him. If it is not feasible for you to closet yourself with him, you will need to have set periods of time to spend alone together, plus be on call at any hour of the day or night.

Keep telling the alcoholic that you have an undying faith in his ability to stop drinking. When he says he can't, assure him that he can. When he isn't able to muster up another hopeful thought, you do it for him. You have to believe in him enough to carry him over the rough spots. Tell him repeatedly that you know he will succeed. Build his self-confidence by letting him know you trust him. It is tremendously important for him to have a friend who cares about what he is doing.

The more you encourage him, the harder he will try. This is part of the pressure that is greater than the desire to drink. The recovering alcoholic is extremely vulnerable and at this point cannot handle any criticisms or negative comments—his or yours. Don't let him condemn himself or converse about the past. Insist that he forget how things used to be. Assure him that he does not have to do everything right; that all he can do at this moment is stay sober. Remind him of the progress he has already made. He is trying to stop, when a week ago he would not have done even that.

Be patient. Because the alcoholic's mind is so muddled, he will not understand as well as most adults would when you are talking with him or trying to explain something. Approach him as you would a child who is learning something for the first time. After all, he has never successfully sobered up before. Don't be solicitous or talk down to him, but speak simply and unemotionally.

Be tolerant of his changing moods. His body is undergoing an enormous physical upheaval. Expect and help him identify his cravings. He will trust you completely if you are patient and he senses that you won't reject him.

Be kind. Kindness is not pity, although some people confuse the two. The literal definition of kindness is doing what is beneficial for someone else. Sometimes kindness demands softness, other times it calls for severity.

You are being kind if you get up in the middle of the night and make coffee, warm milk, or hot soup for the alcoholic because he is having trouble sleeping and is not sure whether he can make it until morning without a drink. A cup of tea and kindness may help him sleep so he can get the rest that is vital to his recovery.

Kindness may also mean telling him he is weak, a coward running from reality, or kidding himself. A kind counselor keeps the drinker on the right track, not letting him dwell on the past or make excuses for himself. You are kind if you don't let him lie to you and if you call a spade a spade. You do what is best for him, not what is easy or comfortable.

Once an alcoholic opens up and starts confiding in you, you must *listen carefully.* Talking relieves his guilt. As you listen, you will be able to pinpoint the onset of cravings and help him identify them and ward them off. You can evaluate his progress and define what stage of withdrawal he's experiencing.

Stages of Withdrawal

There are six stages of withdrawal.

1. The first stage is fear. A cold, gripping panic sets in as the alcoholic realizes he has committed himself to going without the drug and that he may fail.

2. The second stage is denial. He decides, then tries to convince himself and his counselor, that he is not a problem drinker; that their assessment of the situation is wrong and that they are making more of it than is fair or necessary.

3. The third stage is anger. The alcoholic becomes very irate. During this phase he is angry at everyone— his parents for conceiving him, his wife for marrying him, his children for being born, his boss for expecting him to work, and at society for being such a rotten institution. He hates anyone he thinks has contributed to his problem.

Mostly he is angry with himself because he was weak enough to become addicted and because he still wants to drink. He will probably be verbally abusive at this time and may even lash out by kicking objects, throwing things, or pounding his fists on a table or the wall. He needs to be physically active during this stage.

4. Once the anger subsides he is overwhelmed by depression, the fourth stage. When this hits he will alternate moods—experiencing feelings of hopelessness, bitterness, guilt, remorse, and self-pity. It is during this time he is most likely to give up and may be suicidal. Whereas his anger will probably be short-lived, the depression will last for hours or even days.

5. The fifth stage is helplessness when the alcoholic admits the total truth about himself and realizes there is nothing he can do to change what has happened. This is a turning point because it is the time when he also realizes that he can control his future if he chooses to do so.

He acknowledges that he is helpless if he uses alcohol, that he will always be addicted to it and victimized by it but his mind is also clear enough by now for him to understand that he can change if he permanently forsakes liquor.

6. The final stage of withdrawal is hope. The drinker is finally able to visualize and sense what his life can be like if he stays sober. The intense physical pain is subsiding; he is thinking more clearly; his senses are keener than they have been since he started drinking. Tomorrow becomes a promise rather than a problem.

An alcoholic is accustomed to being ignored. People

stopped listening to his drunken ramblings a long time ago. They tuned him out and are turned off by him. As you listen you are affirming to him that what he says matters. Don't register shock at anything he tells you. He may use you as a surrogate priest, confessing sin upon sin, dumping guilt after guilt, spewing out anxiety and shame, and sometimes obscenities. No matter what you hear, don't flinch, pull back or make value judgments.

Once he starts talking about his drinking problem you probably won't be able to stop him. Those of us who have been through this have a standing joke that the truth, once we started telling it, made our tongues a lot looser than the booze ever did. Talking and being listened to is like lancing an emotional and spiritual abscess. Once the wound is open, the poison pours out and the patient experiences tremendous relief. A great pressure is lifted and healing begins.

Sometimes the newspaper will carry a story about how a man or woman saved another person's life. When this happens, all of us smile and are comforted by the fact that in our detached society there are still those out there who care enough to risk their personal well-being to help a brother or sister in need. You may never make the headlines, but if you know someone who has a problem with alcohol and are willing to devote the time and effort, you may be the one to save his life as surely as if you had rescued him from an armed robber or pushed him from in front of a moving vehicle.

Thousands of years ago Cain chided the Lord with a question that has plagued mankind since it was uttered: "Am I my brother's keeper?" (Gen. 4:9). God did not respond with a cut-and-dried yes or no but eventually sent His own beloved Son to save us all. Christ cared for the sick and outcast, had compassion on all people, and suffered beyond our comprehension so that we could become whole. Jesus answered Cain's question with His life. He was His brother's keeper. We can do no less than contribute in the same way if we want to live full, abundant lives that are reflective of His divine nature.

Notes
1. Betty Ford, *The Times of My Life* (New York: Harper and Row Publishers, 1978), p. 281.
2. Joyce Brothers, "Joan Kennedy's Road Back from Alcoholism," *Good Housekeeping,* April 1979, p. 114.
3. Ford, *Times of My Life,* p. 287.

nine
The Fractured Family

Anytime someone in a family has a terminal illness, all the members are affected; no one likes to see someone they love suffer. They feel frustrated or guilty that they cannot help alleviate the other person's pain. They may worry that they inadvertently caused or intensified the sickness. Anger is not an uncommon reaction when someone is terminally ill. Fear is prevalent in the survivors because their security and life-style are threatened by the death of a loved one.

The stress of watching someone suffer and die causes problems among the various family members. Relationships are strained because abnormal demands are made on each person's time, energy, and emotions. All normal living patterns are disrupted. Resentments build, tempers flare. And under it all is the selfish grief each individual experiences as he faces his own personal loss.

A Family Disease

Alcoholism is a terminal disease that affects the entire family.

A co-alcoholic is one, usually a family member, who has been engulfed by the life-style of an alcoholic. His life revolves around the mood and drinking pattern of the alcoholic. Whether obvious or subtle, the co-alcoholic's life and behavior are dominated by the alcoholic's manipulation.[1] Along with normal reactions to illness as described above, co-alcoholics suffer in the following ways.

Families of alcoholics face *shame, failure and embarrassment* because their mother's, father's, sister's, brother's, aunt's, uncle's, or cousin's illness is self-induced. Poor old Ralph couldn't help that he got bone cancer. Dad's heart attack, Mother's stroke, are socially acceptable ways to go. But it is degrading and humiliating when someone you love is dying from over-consumption of alcohol. The "alcoholic" family is a fractured family—broken, split, fragmented—going in different directions and working at cross purposes.

They feel *rejected.* One reason families of alcoholics are doubly hurt is because they feel that if the drinker cared enough for them, loved them the way he should, he wouldn't drink. So they sense deep rejection, having been deserted by their loved one for a bottle of booze.

Another reason is that they are *totally helpless.* They can't say, "Why don't you go to the doctor and see what he can give you for your drinking?" they way they could say, "Why don't you go to the doctor and get that cough (or shortness of breath or that lump in your breast) checked out?" They are impotent.

Consequently, the family of an alcoholic will be as adversely affected by his disease as the alcoholic himself and they *must also be rehabilitated.* They must also go through a recovery process. They need to be treated and healed too. It is my personal opinion that any family that has gone through the disease will need therapy. Let me explain why.

When the alcoholic was drinking he *destroyed all faith* the family members had in him. The intimate, cohesive trust relationship that binds families, that makes blood thicker than water, was totally severed. So when the alcoholic says he is going to quit drinking, his family looks upon that statement as just another lie. Even when he stops, they still don't believe him.

Not only have family members lost faith in the alcoholic, they have *lost faith in each other.* Children cannot understand why they have been neglected or abused or why their sober parent let the drunken one act as he or she did. Or, the nondrinking parent has had to side against his or her spouse, to protect the children. So each person is emotionally isolated from the other.

No relationship can thrive without trust. There is no way the individuals in the family can function as a unit unless they can trust one another. And they cannot communicate well enough to rebuild their mutual faith without the aid of an objective outsider.

Living in a home where one of the authority figures (husband or wife, father or mother) is an alcoholic is like being employed at a company where the boss is always drunk. There is no management, no ultimate chain of command. Roles are not established and there are no set guidelines about whom to turn to for what.

Because they have had to operate autonomously and fend for themselves for so long, *children are resentful* and have a difficult time adjusting to the authority of a rehabilitating parent. As a matter of fact, children of alcoholics have trouble accepting authority of any kind because a person who was supposed to have cared for them, directed and guided their lives, and protected them, abdicated the position. They have learned not to rely on the adults closest to them, so are rebellious and defensive toward all authority figures.

I know this is true with my own children. They do not respect my position as their mother because for so long I did not do what a mother should. They much more readily accept Jon's authority than they do mine. I know that is because when I was drunk I was so inconsistent and unreasonable that they couldn't respond to what I asked of them. So, unless they wanted to mind me, they didn't, and I was too drunk to care anyway.

Reestablishing my rightful, God-given position as their mother has not been easy; I haven't succeeded yet. I have literally had to make them follow through on instructions I give or things I ask them to do. When they don't want to do something I ask them to do, they ignore me, as they did so often when I was drunk. They pretend not to hear me or act as if I am not in the room.

I insist on eye-to-eye contact when we talk because they were so accustomed to tuning out my drunken ramblings that they still don't listen to me very well. That is one of the many penalties I have paid for my alcoholism.

The Problem of Abusiveness

Alcoholics are abusive. We may not all beat our children or spouses but we say and do cruel things when we are drunk. And many problem drinkers do physically abuse family members.

Drunken husbands frequently *hit or sexually abuse their wives.* When I spoke to some women in a battered wives group, the majority of them agreed that their husbands had been drinking before they physically assaulted them or their children. Most of the women were certain that their husbands were alcoholics. Many of them have been permanently scarred both in body and mind.

Sometimes a parent will *batter his children* when he is too drunk to know what he is doing. Some physical abuse is unintentional but is equally as dangerous and debilitating as if it was intentional. Drunken parents, whose reflexes are slowed by booze, drop infants, stumble into children, or fall on them.

As I interviewed children and teenagers, everyone I talked to told me they had been physically hurt by their alcoholic parent. Some had been purposely mistreated but some were injured unintentionally. One girl told me how, when she was six years old, her father came to kiss her goodnight and passed out when he bent over the bed, fell on her and almost suffocated her before her mother could pull him off. She still panics when he gets too close to her.

Family members also suffer *gross mental abuse*. The adult who is psychologically warped from use of the drug inflicts his sickness on his family. The results are devastating. The family has to overcome both the example the alcoholic set and the stigma that was stamped on them. I cringe and want to weep when I think of the embarrassment I caused the people I love.

Children dread being embarrassed by their parents, but the poor kid whose mother or father is a drunk lives with it constantly. One girl told me that she decided it was better not to have friends than to have them and be embarrassed in front of them by her parent's drunken remarks or irrational behavior.

Some teenagers are so ashamed and guilty about

their parent's alcoholism that they become withdrawn. They simply do not make friends. They don't want anyone to pity them or laugh at them. They don't want to have to explain why they can't bring classmates home or make plans with the other kids, so they don't develop any close relationships.

The embarrassment isn't limited to children. Wives and husbands of alcoholics get the brunt of it, too. One lady told me that after her husband showed up drunk at her place of business several times, acting loud and garish, that her boss told her he thought it would be better if she resigned. He explained that her work was above average and that he was terribly sorry but that he could not have his office disrupted. Out of sheer embarrassment she left, without trying to defend herself. She said she felt as if she deserved to be fired because she was not able to stop her husband from drinking.

The Tendency Toward Alcoholism

Down through history, statistics have shown that alcoholism runs in families. Recent studies tend to support the genetic theory. Research done by Dr. Donald W. Goodwin, at the University of Kansas Medical Center, Kansas City, shows that "children of alcoholics are particularly vulnerable to alcoholism whether raised by parents or nonalcoholic foster parents," and that familial alcoholism is evident when one or more close relatives of an alcoholic are also alcoholics.[2]

He further found that heredity may be a factor (1) when there is a family history of alcoholism, (2) when there is an early onset of the disease, (3) when severe symptoms require treatment at an early age, and (4) at the absence of other conspicuous psychopathology.

This does not mean, however, that all alcoholics have an inherited tendency toward the disease. Such proof is far from conclusive. Environment is still the dominant factor. Early in the book I shared how my home setting and my parents' attitudes affected my drinking. Children learn more from what they see than from what they are told.

Sadly, children of alcoholics imitate their parents' behavior. One elementary school-age boy told me that he beat up on the kids at school all the time because his father beat up on him when he got drunk, which was quite often. Although the boy hated the fact that his father drank, he was already unconsciously imitating his father's actions, and will most likely continue doing so into adulthood, including drinking as his father does.

The sixteen-year-old daughter of an alcoholic father told me how much she hated that her father had been drinking all of her life. Now she is drinking and said that although she knows where it will lead she can't seem to stop herself. She said it as if she has been brainwashed. "I have all the same excuses for drinking that my father had but it doesn't matter." Like does beget like.

Recuperation and Recovery

Despite all this, there is hope for the "alcoholic" family, even if the alcoholic is still drinking. I recommend that families of problem drinkers go to their local Al-Anon chapter. The organization is a support group for families of alcoholics and is affiliated with Alcoholics Anonymous. They can teach husbands, wives and children how to live with a drunk and survive.

For those families who are fortunate enough to be living with a rehabilitating alcoholic, I suggest the following procedures.

1. **Get involved in family therapy with an organization, psychologist, or church of your choice.** Call your city or county mental health organization if you don't

know where to start. If you prefer, contact a pastor, rabbi, or priest; but every family member needs help, individually and collectively.

If the person you first contact cannot help you, keep trying until someone can. While I was counseling the wife and five children of an alcoholic man, I asked them if they ever sought help anywhere. The children said they didn't want to hurt their mother or embarrass her by asking anyone for help. One of them said he might have asked their priest for help. I called their priest and asked what his response would have been. He replied, "I don't know how to counsel anyone who has alcoholism as a problem. I probably would refer them to an organization formed for that purpose." Perhaps this book would be a good gift for such a person.

2. Establish family routines—mealtimes, bedtimes, dates for outings—and then do not let anything interfere with keeping them. Knowing what is going to happen and when it will take place, then carrying through with plans, builds trust and a secure atmosphere.

3. Become personally accountable to one another. Children should ask permission to go anyplace—even if it is outside to play. This may seem like a little thing but they are not used to checking in or being responsible to the alcoholic parent and that has to change. In "normal" homes, children are expected to communicate with their parents about their whereabouts.

Likewise, teenagers and adults should let other family members know where they are going and what time they will return; and they must call if they are detained or their plans change. Not only is this courteous but it eliminates anxiety and says, "I care enough about you to tell you where I am." It also teaches responsibility.

4. Be openly affectionate. Love covers a multitude

of sins. A family that has been separated by alcoholism needs to make contact. Hug one another, kiss each other. Say I love you. Tousle heads, hold hands, sit close. Touch. Praise one another and do favors for each other. Emotional closeness is a by-product of physical closeness.

5.   Above all, be honest with one another. The "alcoholic" family has lived in a maze of lies. The alcoholic has manipulated and lied to everyone. Children pretend not to know what is happening when a mother or father drinks, so they lie to themselves and to others about their parent's behavior. Husbands and wives excuse the drunken spouse by lying about what he does. Many families of alcoholics pretend the drinker doesn't have a problem. Lying, deceit, and self-delusion are preconditioned habits.

If trust is going to be reestablished, it has to be based on truth. It won't be easy for the family to tell the truth about everything, but they must try. It would be wise to have a family conference and discuss the problem and lay some ground rules. Talk about the kinds of lies each one told in the past, why they told them, and why dishonesty is harmful. Then decide what your family can do to change.

6. Finally, the recovering family should plan to spend time together as a unit with the Lord. They don't have to be religious to do this. They may want to go to church, mass, or temple together or they might pick a time every other day or so when they get together to pray and read the Bible. It doesn't have to be formal or long but they need to acknowledge, as a group, their dependence on God and each other.

Jon and I are spending a half-hour a day reading the Gospels. Neither of us knew much about the Bible when we started, but a friend gave us a study Bible, so we read a chapter, read the footnotes, and talk about what the Scripture means to us. Now we are starting to do this with the children. I know if the Lord could deprogram me He can do the same for them.

There will always be scars because there were deep wounds, but scars also mean there has been healing. With God's help, the fractured family can be put together again. They can become whole.

Notes
1. In my book on co-alcoholism to be published by Regal Books, I have covered in-depth the role of the active co-alcoholic and his or her road to recovery.
2. Beverly Beyette, "Alcoholic Women Get In-Home Help," *Los Angeles Times*, September 9, 1979, "View" section.

ten
Does It Ever End?

I was frantic. Jon and I had talked until he was so exhausted he couldn't stay awake any longer. I had paced the floor, smoked so many cigarettes my mouth was sore, and drunk so much tea my insides sloshed when I walked.

I had prayed—desperately pleading with God to ease the agitation I was feeling, to lift the anxiety and anger I was experiencing. Nothing was working! I wanted a drink. I had to have one. I wanted to drown the hurt and indignation that had been inflicted on me by someone I loved and trusted very much.

I glanced at the clock. I knew I wouldn't make it through the night. It was 1:30 A.M. when I picked up the phone and called Jo. "Help me! I'm having horrible cravings," I cried. "I won't make it through the night. I don't know what to do. Talk to me—"

Does it ever end? I wish I could tell you it does, but it doesn't. The preceding tense episode happened when Jo and I were starting to work on the last chapter of this book. Two people I care about who affect me negatively got a foothold in my life again. This couple, for many years, has been emotionally detrimental to me, drained me of my self-esteem, and detracted from my dignity. As a result of renewed personal contact with them I regressed to where I had been right after I stopped drinking.

I was torn, irrational, creating cravings yet not seeing them for what they were. I was fighting pain I knew could be dulled with alcohol, frightened half out of my mind that I was losing control. *But I didn't drink!* How appropriately ironic that God would choose that way to refresh my memory and at the same time prove to me that what I have shared with you is true. No, it never ends. But it does not have to control you once you have taken charge of your life.

During this last struggle I spent many hours on the phone talking to Jo and shouting, "Why?" at God. I cried a lot, which is unusual for me. Jo told me I was suffering through this hurtful situation the way "normal" people do; that for the first time in many years I was going through an emotional upheaval the way most people do; experiencing the pain and weakness all human beings feel when they have been hurt, attacked, or rejected. In other words, I was feeling things I had always before dulled with indulgence in alcohol.

Does it ever end? This summer my doctor discovered that I have a severe hormone imbalance which can be easily corrected with medication. Although I got the prescription filled, I was afraid to take the pills. It wasn't until I suffered from regular fainting spells, passed out on the stairs and almost broke my neck that I consented to take the medication.

Why? I am desperately afraid of drugs and will do anything I can to keep from taking them. I know there is a possibility that if I regularly and systematically put a pill into my mouth and rely on whatever is in it to make me feel better, that next I may swallow a glass of booze when I need relief. I know hundreds of thousands of women take artificial hormones, but I am terrified at the thought of relying on any drug, ever, for any reason.

No, it never ends. Recently I had a kidney infection. I had severe pain but could not take even a mild narcotic to ease my discomfort. I made it through the illness without taking so much as an aspirin. I know if I pop one pill into my mouth, seeking artificial relief and comfort, it can awaken old desires and cravings. I dare not risk reverting to old habit patterns by relying on any drug. My alcoholism is a more dangerous disease than a kidney infection. The pain was bad, but it was better than booze, and I won!

Do you know how I won in these situations? Certainly not by being superhuman. I won by doing what I have advised in this book. In doing so, I proved to myself that I am rehabilitated.

Dry Alcoholics

Strange as it may sound, there are people who stop drinking and, although they don't drink anymore, are not rehabilitated. They are what I call dry alcoholics. They are the ones who substitute something else for the booze and never get on with their lives. A dry alcoholic overcomes the addiction to the drug but he never conquers the cravings nor his reliance on artificial sources. He never faces reality, but retreats into something more acceptable than liquor to solve his drinking problem.

Let me illustrate. I know of one man who stopped drinking ten years ago—but he is a dry alcoholic, not rehabilitated. When he relinquished alcohol, his wife and children were thrilled. They thought he would become a new man, one with whom they could communicate, who would relate to them as husband and father, take an interest in their lives. Sadly, the only thing that changed was that he quit drinking.

Instead of retreating into a bottle he has substituted television and crossword puzzles for booze. He comes home at night, turns on the tube and, other than at dinner time, sits and stares at program after program while doing crossword puzzles.

He does not talk to his family. He refuses to get involved in the everyday affairs of life. He is still as tuned out to the needs and emotions of those around him as he was when he was drinking. Only now, his wife and children are more frustrated because their needs are still not being met but they cannot criticize a sloppy drunk. They are neglected because the husband and father watches too much television.

Yet, the dark side of his nature—his trigger temper, his lack of compassion, his critical attitudes, his unreasonable demands, his selfishness—still dominates his personality. He quit drinking but he has not changed. He is still as sick as he was when he was falling-down drunk.

Jo has a friend who dried out more than fourteen years ago. He became a "workaholic." He devotes himself entirely to his career. He has given his wife and children material luxuries and, to all outward appearances, he is a good husband and father. But within the family structure there is no communication or closeness.

This man has not faced reality but has secluded himself safely in his job and uses it the way he once used liquor. He is still shut off from truth, still has severe psychological problems, and still inflicts unhappiness on himself and those who love him. He is not well. And he could return to the bottle at any moment.

Obviously, in many ways, a dry alcoholic is easier to live with than a drunk one, but he has not been restored to fullness of life. Dry alcoholics still have a long way to go in the rehabilitative process; yet, I would venture to say that since they stopped drinking they are ignored. That is because we see drunkenness, not the disease of alcoholism, as the problem. So when symptoms subside we automatically assume the problem is gone too. However, that is not true.

People who live with dry alcoholics are faced with the same set of problems they had before the drinker overcame his physical addiction to alcohol. They know that the abusiveness is merely repackaged when the drinking stops.

What can you do if you know, live with, or are married to a dry alcoholic?

1. **The first step, of course, is to recognize that the person is not rehabilitating.** Not drinking is only a small part of recovering from alcoholism. It is, as I have previously discussed, the first and obviously a necessary one, but it is not the only or final one.

If an alcoholic is rehabilitating, those close to him will know. Certainly the changes may come slowly and often he will slip backward one step for every two he takes forward, but he will make progress.

2. **The next step is to approach the dry alcoholic as you would one who is drinking.** In whatever way your individual situation demands, tell him the truth about what he is doing and point out patterns and cravings that make him retreat to the booze substitute.

The wife whose husband retreated behind the television set would actually turn it off, take the pencil and puzzle book out of her husband's hands and tell him one of the children needed to talk to him. When he would angrily refuse she would remind him that he was acting the same way he acted when he was drinking.

3. Another step in helping a dry alcoholic is to refuse to accept the alcohol substitute as a satisfactory solution. Just because a problem drinker replaces booze with something we would call good or acceptable does not mean it is. The wife of the workaholic would have to inform her husband that his being gone eighteen hours a day at the office leaves her no less lonely than when he was gone eighteen hours a day on a binge.

No, it never ends. Some alcoholics never go beyond physically drying out, although if they are made aware of the problem they probably can. Others attack life with zeal and hope. But all of us have to deal with this one predominant question every day of our lives: Where do I go from here?

What Next?

Probably the greatest, most immediate concern an alcoholic has when he stops drinking—after he gets through that intense first month or so—is how to live his life. He has been living abnormally for so long he has forgotten what is normal. He wonders, What next? He is apprehensive and frightened.

He is plagued by "what ifs." What if he's invited to dinner at the boss's house and wine is served with dinner? What if he goes to a party and the smell of booze whets his addictive appetite? What if he walks into the supermarket one day and cannot get past the beer display? He can drive himself crazy with "what ifs."

A little advance planning can alleviate a lot of anxiety. If an alcoholic is going to live a normal life he must accept the fact that everywhere he goes he will be faced with liquor. Drinking is not merely socially acceptable but is an ingrained part of our cultural etiquette. "Good hosts" always serve drinks. Nondrinkers are considered weird or are sometimes categorized as religious fanatics or health nuts. And since the alcoholic is a nondrinker, he might as well adjust to the fact that many people will think he is strange or socially maladjusted. Examined in the light of how he behaved when he was drinking, it is the preferable form of maladjustment.

I planned ahead. I made up a system for rejecting alcohol in social settings. If I am offered a drink, I simply say no thanks then ask for a nonalcoholic beverage. Some of the mineral waters are as fashionable as booze these days. Its "chic" and "in" to ask for lime and tonic, club soda, or Perrier water. If I am pushed I merely say, "I cannot drink. I am an alcoholic." I have found that, contrary to what I feared, most people respect my strength and courage and don't pity me at all.

I am not ashamed to admit that I am an alcoholic. I am proud that I no longer drink. This openness also helps me stay sober. Once people know I have a problem I no longer feel pressured to be anything but myself and nobody tries to push me into taking a drink. They respect my abstinence.

In addition to having a strategy to rely on when the unexpected happens, *having someone to turn to also* helps relieve fear and tension in the recovering alcoholic. He always needs—and I stress *always*—someone to dump on. Visits with a friend or counselor are therapeutic. Such rap sessions where the alcoholic reevaluates his progress and vents his failures and frustrations are the hands that hold him if he starts slipping.

In the brief ordeal I described at the first of this chapter, as I talked with Jo I realized I wasn't behaving abnormally by ranting, crying, hurting, and being angry. If I had not had her to confide in I could have decided I wasn't supposed to act that way or have such feelings, and out of guilt I might have resorted to the bottle. Talking helped me maintain my perspective and my sanity.

The alcoholic should share with his friend or counselor about anything that bothers him enough to interfere with the rehabilitation program he has set up for himself. He shouldn't use a family member because it is difficult to be totally open and objective with them. They have their own set of fears and frustrations about his recovery and in some cases he needs to talk about conflicts within the family; so it is impossible for relatives to help. They are threatened. They get defensive. They need help in recovering from the effects of alcoholism.

But the alcohlic must have someone in whom he can confide. If he does not, the emotions, resentments and anxieties he bottles up inside can reappear in the form of cravings. When I am personally working with alcoholics, I establish a routine and suggest we set a particular time each day to make contact. Then, if something upsetting happens during the day, they have that meeting to look forward to and can maintain their sobriety until we talk. I become an accountability factor.

No, It Never Ends

Even though it never ends, it does diminish. Fortunately, alcoholism is a disease that can be arrested by the person who has it. Other illnesses rely on outside help. Diabetics must have insulin. Cancer can be treated in a number of ways, as can heart disease. But an alcoholic cannot take a medication, have surgery, radiation treatments, or chemotherapy. He has to willfully stop drinking to rid himself of the disease.

We have already established that once a person is an alcoholic he will always be one. He will also always have to live with the residual by-products of that alcoholism. He has to adjust to the physical results, such as the damage his body suffered during the binges and drinking bouts. There is also the emotional trauma; he has scars on his soul. He must live with the fact that even those closest to him have lost faith in him and will find it exceedingly difficult to trust him.

For example, certain people who know about my past sometimes are suspicious of my actions. When I'm tired, grumpy, angry, or wiped out emotionally for some reason, they think I might be drinking. During the first few years of my recovery I was greeted with a note of caution whenever I was late getting home.

Kids tend to be skeptics the longest. Until just recently, my children would coyly sample my drinks to see if there was booze in them. We are still paying a price as a family for some financial fiascos I was involved in when I was drinking. We have poor credit because I wrote so many bad checks, ran up such large debts, and spent the household money on liquor rather than paying the bills.

I have to be doubly careful when I drive because I have been arrested on a 502 (drunk driving). I live daily with the effects of the emotional damage my children suffered when I was neglecting them. But time alleviates much of this and gradually life balances out.

Could It Happen to You?

Do you think you could ever be vulnerable enough to become an alcoholic? Or, are you like most of us who delude ourselves into thinking that such things only happen to "the other guy"? None of us likes to believe we are the one who will have the automobile accident, whose house will be burglarized, or who will be raped or robbed. We don't like to admit we are susceptible to the multitude of evils that plague mankind.

Just the other day I had lunch with a woman who told me alcohol could never be a problem for her, then she drank two double margaritas before we ate. She was tipsy before the food came.

There are *ten million* alcoholics in the United States today. For every one of them there are three others affected. This means that *forty million* Americans currently are affected by the disease of alcoholism. Yes, it could happen to you. In a broad, general sense, everyone is a candidate. Some people are more susceptible than others, but if anyone indulges long enough and consumes enough liquor, he can become addicted to alcohol. And if there is a genetic predisposition, some of you may not need quantity to perpetrate the onset of the disease.

Of those ten million alcoholics in this country, some are like me—they were hooked very early in life but did not know enough to pay attention to the warning signs. Some delude themselves by thinking they need a drink to help them slow down and to bring some sense and peace into their lives. Some only drink socially—but they socialize all the time so they have a reason to drink.

There are those teenagers who imitate their parents or give in to peer pressure and drink because it's the "in" thing to do—then they find they can't stop. Young housewives who feel neglected, bored, or unfulfilled are prime targets. Religious people, Christians who openly voice the horrors of alcohol and intemperance, are often closet drinkers who are forced to hide their problem rather than seek help because they know they will be condemned and ostracized rather than loved and helped by their church.

Women are particularly vulnerable at this time in history. Dr. Terry Davis of UCLA says research statistics show that there are specific family patterns that cause women to become alcoholics: " . . . isolation in the home, protection by the family and the failure or unwillingness of others to recognize the illness." She is convinced that "we really don't want to see alcoholism in women, especially in young women."[1] So the problem grows.

The National Institute of Drug Abuse says that in the last twenty-five years the number of women alcoholics has increased by double the rate of men. This figure may be even higher because women hide their drinking problems more than do men. The institute reports, "While society tends to accept the fact of alcohol abuse in men, women's problems are neither accepted nor tolerated. Instead, they are labelled unfit, weak, fallen, often by themselves as well as the world at large."[2]

Recent studies conducted by Dr. Benjamin Morgan Jones, of the University of Oklahoma department of psychiatry and behavioral sciences, show that most men require nearly twice as much alcohol to get drunk as women, and become intoxicated more slowly, because men have less fatty tissue and more water content in their bodies. Since fat does not absorb alcohol and water dilutes it, a drink will enter a woman's bloodstream faster and affect her more rapidly and severely than it will a man. So a given amount of alcohol has a more intense and immediate effect on a woman than on a man.

Signs to Watch For

How can you tell if you or someone you know is easing into alcoholism? There are many warning signs but they are easily overlooked because they happen so gradually and are such an ingrained part of our culture.

A teenager doesn't start drinking a quart of vodka a day. He probably starts with a beer. Just one. And because everybody does it and it is harmless kid fun, the parents chalk it up to youth, and ignore the growing set of symptoms. The businessman has a couple of drinks with lunch every day and a cocktail or two before dinner. The housewife relaxes with a wine cooler in the middle of the afternoon and puts a jigger of brandy in her after-dinner coffee. Who is going to question these seemingly innocuous actions?

Yet in many instances they are much more than that. They are danger signals. All of us should be more aware of the needs of those closest to us and be available to communicate with those we love and care about. We must watch and be willing to admit the severity of behavior which, on the surface, appears to be harmless and even socially acceptable.

Here are some basic, general symptoms of alcoholism to watch for. These may not all be present in each person but usually most of them will be.

1. Increased alcohol/drug intake. A person who is leaning toward becoming a problem drinker may become excessive in his consumption of other drugs, such as aspirin, vitamins, or tranquilizers. He may drink more coffee and soft drinks than usual to get a lift from the stimulation of caffeine.

2. Emergence of set drinking patterns. Someone who is drinking too much will drink at specific intervals and may even drink only with certain people and in a set place. Watch for anyone who has to have a drink at a certain time each day.

3. Personality changes. If a person who is usually uptight becomes hang-loose and relaxed with no apparent effort on his part to evoke such changes, he may be drinking. So might the perfectionist who doesn't care anymore, the introvert who suddenly becomes a charming extrovert or the even-tempered person who has become sullen and argumentative. Any marked personality change that is not caused by some notable reason might be perpetrated by excessive drinking.

4. Slowing of physical and emotional responses. Dulled reactions are an obvious sign of drinking. An alcoholic can actually physically hurt himself quite badly and not respond to the pain until the narcosis of the liquor wears off.

A heavy drinker moves and reacts more slowly than a nondrinker. He is unsteady on his feet and his responses and sense of awareness are subdued by the depressant he is ingesting. Frequently, his speech will be slurred, although he is not aware of his thick tongue.

5. Forgetfulness. Alcohol dulls the brain and impairs the thinking process. So, if someone regularly forgets appointments, important dates, misplaces papers or car keys, and is not as involved in his own life as he used to be, he may be drinking.

6. Letting down of normal performance standards. Teachers say they can tell when teenagers in their classes are drinking because their grades slip markedly. The man or woman, who generally does an average or good job but suddenly becomes slipshod and uncaring about his or her work could be drinking.

Things that used to matter to them, such as a job well done, don't matter any more. They lower their expectations and blame others—family members, colleagues, the boss—for their failures and sloppy performance. Drinking alters their values.

7. Schedule changes. The alcoholic who is trying to hide his drinking problem has to devise ways and places to drink. In order to do this he disrupts his schedule. The person who looks for ways and reasons to get out of the house, who drums up excuses for leaving, who becomes involved with a new set of friends or a multitude of outside activities may be manipulating so he can go somewhere to drink.

Staying late at the office for sudden, unexpected business meetings that last into the night hours, when this has never been the case before, are symptoms which might indicate a drinking problem.

Usually these warning signs operate in conjunction with one another. If a husband has to stay late at the office for several nights, it does not mean he is drinking. But if he is continually kept away from home for a variety of reasons, when this was not his previous pattern, and he is also forgetful, complaining of headaches and taking large doses of aspirin and having an Alka Seltzer with his morning coffee, he may have a problem. These are things of which we should all be aware. Early detection may save years of misery.

Freedom from Alcohol

The alcoholic's world is one of constant danger. He lives in fear of being discovered. Although he may not realize it, he is risking his life when he drinks then drives, or when he messes up on the job. He is a potential killer when he gets behind the wheel of an automobile. His health is constantly in jeopardy.

Before I stopped drinking I was totally enslaved to the habit. Drinking wasn't something I did, it was my life-style. I couldn't make plans because I did not know if I could follow through on them. I might be drunk when I was supposed to show up for an appointment. Or, I was very careful about what invitations I accepted because I would not go anyplace unless I was sure I could get a drink when I got there. I never knew from one moment to the next what was going to happen to me or what it would cost. I was totally at the mercy of the booze.

Now, I am free. I can go anywhere and not have to worry about fighting the crowd for drinks. I am healthier and my mind and body belong to me. I am proud of myself. I can hold my head high instead of cowering in the corner with a glass of Bourbon.

My greatest blessing is the way my family feels about me. My husband treats me like I am the most wonderful woman who ever lived. My children admire me now. They no longer make remarks about my drinking but joyfully and proudly tell people I'm an author. And the fear is gone from their eyes. Our lives aren't perfect—we have a lot of restructuring left to do—but we are united in love as never before.

I am so grateful that God responded when I called on Him for help. It has only been through His strength that I can claim victory over alcoholism. I got a second chance. God was gracious to me and I have learned how to be good to myself so I can count in the lives of those I love. I am alive. I am here today, in the now, contributing to this world in which I live. I am an alcoholic, but I am healthy, I am happy and I am free. How good it is!

YOU DO HAVE TO CHOOSE

There's so much love inside us
It screams to get out,
A silently deafening desperate shout.

Though no one can hear it
The signs are all there.
If you shout it, they'll hear it
And someone will care.

You may have to knock
On just one more door.
And if one door is closing,
You knock on one more.

Love keeps us happy and healthy and sane,
And protects us from garbage
That fogs up our brain.

To have it is your right,
And you won't have to fight.
All that you have to do,
Is to love yourself, too.

So, go out and try it,
What have you to lose?
I've told you the secret,
Now you have to choose.[3]

—Claire Costales

Notes

1. Beverly Beyette, "Alcoholic Women Get In-Home Help," *Los Angeles Times,* September 9, 1979, "View" section.
2. Charles H. Derovner, "More Women Are Looking to Drink," *Valley News and Green Sheet,* August 5, 1979, "Flair" section.
3. "You Do Have to Choose," by Claire Costales © 1980.

Other Regal Books to help you build better relationships